WILLIAM M. BRANHAM
THE SEVEN MYSTERIOUS SEALS AND THE SHARKS

BY THOMAS A. SHORT

FIRST EDITION

Writer's disclaimer:
Distributed by Independent Publishing Groups

This is a work of creative nonfiction. All of the content and events in this collection are true to the best of the author's investigations and memory of sermon quotes by the renown Prophet/Evangelist William M. Branham. Some names may have been changed to protect the identity of certain parties. The author in no way represents any company, corporation, or brand mentioned herein. The views expressed in this collection are solely those of the author.

© COPYRIGHT 2025, Thomas Short
Copyright Registration #TXu 2-457-272

ISBN # 979-889766520-4

First Printing – February 25, 2025

Thomas Short, author, shortfamily10@gmail.com

All photographs on the cover and in the book are provided by the author and the public domain.

Cover and book design by Helen Mullins, hmgraphics@comcast.net

Printed in the U.S.A.

A note of heartfelt appreciation goes out to all those who contributed to the unwavering support and development of this work. I recognize specifically Helen Mullins as editor and format designer of this beautiful book. Thank you all so much.

Thomas A. Short

I·N·T·R·O·D·U·C·T·I·O·N

A country boy raised by a bootlegger father, young William Branham (seven years old) was confronted by a whirlwind in a tree, out of which an angelic voice commanded him to a rigorous life of self-denial and purity. At his eighteenth year he went out west to become a cowboy; running from his calling, he sought out his own destiny. Death struck his father and brother which drove him back to Jeffersonville, Indiana, and to seek after God's purpose. He reconnected with Hope Brumback and a relationship began. He was told while proposing, that she was pregnant and he accepted the responsibility to cover for her, hide the matter and care for the child. The supernatural became apparent as miracles took place and a whirling pillar of fire came down over him (1933) as he was baptizing in the Ohio river. Due to Hope's parents' rejection of fanatical behaviors, by "Pentecostal trash," William remained with the Pentecostal/Baptist church.

The 1937 flood hit the Ohio valley which ended with Hope and her little girl's death. Before she died, she told him to press on to greater experiences with God, regardless of what her parents might say. He agreed. Billy Paul, Hope's first child, was taken to the meetings and nurtured by a young lady named Meda, which William later married. He faithfully withheld family secrets to allow the world to think that the five children born were his own biological offspring.

In 1947, while camping out in his prayer cave an Angel suddenly appeared out of a bright light and spoke to him of his strange life and his future calling. The gifts given him would produce a powerful healing campaign and deliverance to the world. Conflicts grew as the crowds grew around the miraculous Evangelistic meetings. The dead and diseased were pronounced well, the lame and the withered stood whole and the blind eyes were opened.

In 1950 Billy Paul went to bible college (short termed) and his allegiance turned to the upper echelon of religious affairs. Billy Paul's resistance to correction by God's Prophet turned to resentment. He then served God (continuing to follow the meetings) for self-centered gain and promotion. When opportunities arose to best his stepfather, Reverend Branham, he took what he could.

Reverend Branham's ministry and calling to this heavenly vision, was looked upon as irresponsible and heartless, often he was away from family affairs and from wedding anniversaries. The Angel of God had warned him not to try to explain his secretive life, and his remaining aloof from Meda's marriage relationship. The Angel told him if he remained true to the heavenly calling he would be used as the Anointed One, the second coming Messiah. He was taken into heaven to meet those who had went to their rewards. He, unbeknownst to loved ones or friends, transformed into living creatures, one being a huge brown bear which walked out into the hunting party's rifle scopes of Ed Byskal and Billy Paul Branham.

No matter the vindication of the supernatural ministry, Billy Paul refused to submit to his stepfather's gentle corrections and the warnings that the ministers were playing political games and being Ecclesiastical predator sharks.

The World Council of Churches spokeswoman asked those attending the convention, who might know of this "troublemaker," which had dared to stand up to their power. Billy Paul accepted the treacherous role to find "dirty laundry."

After the Angel of God revealed to him the mysterious and "hard to swallow" doctrine contained in the secrets of the Seven Seals now open to him, the theologians had their ammunition to derail Reverend Branham's huge success with the masses. They would twist the doctrine he brought to the people, as a means for the denominational minded folks to ridicule.

After William Branham's exaltation into Deity, he began to form a plan for his departure from the Earth. A sudden secretive escape from death was planned, which otherwise would eliminate his chances as the Kinsman-Redeemer, Messiah. A car accident would take place at his departure and Billy Paul would sell him out as a (common person) which had not received God's full born-again transformation – being a sinner and mortal, destined to die.

The story ends with William Branham translated into an angelic Theophany, dressed as a Native American Indian Chief, riding his supernatural white horse and shouting a message back to the world.

Written by Thomas Short

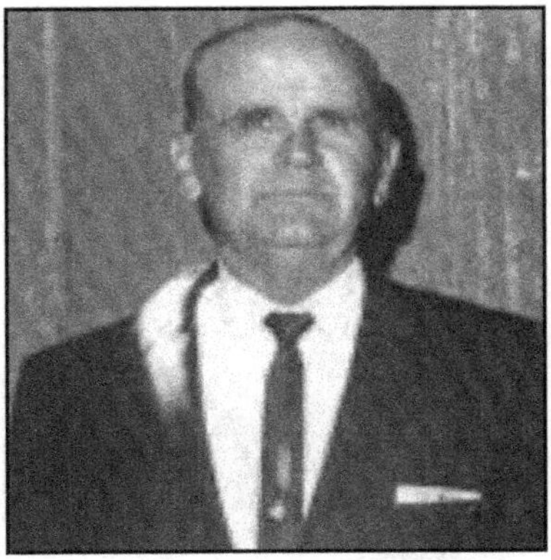

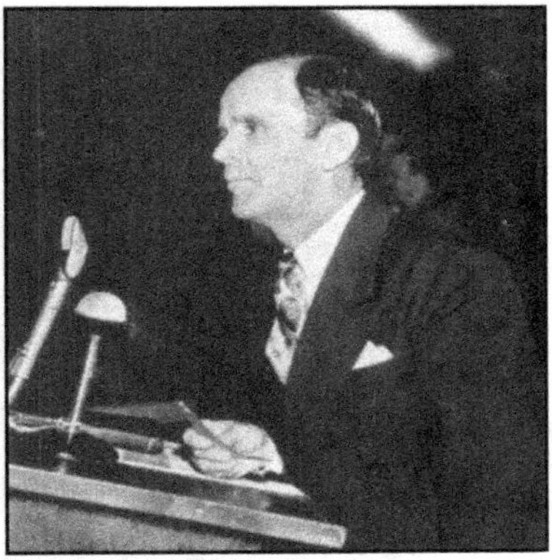

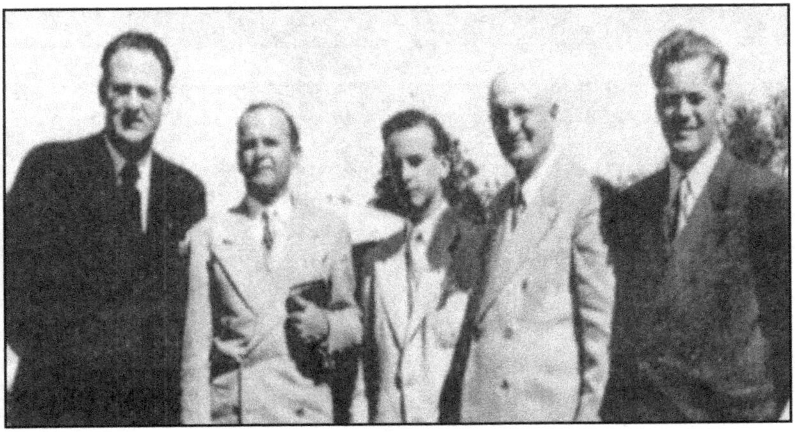

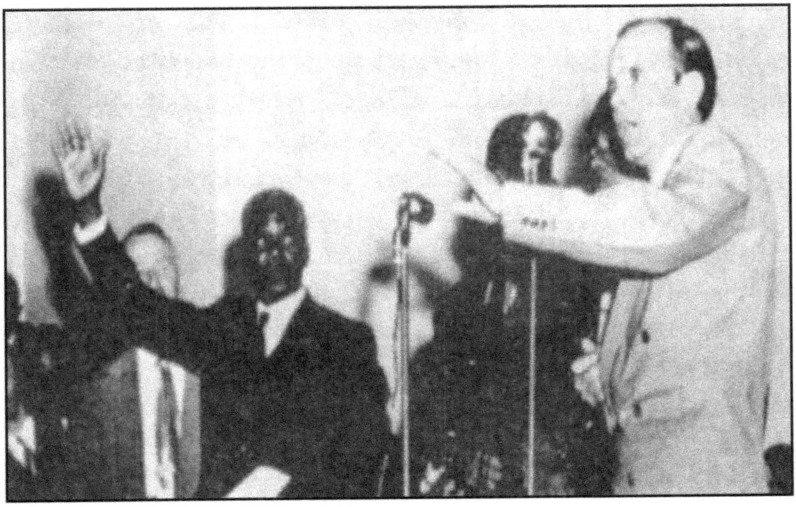

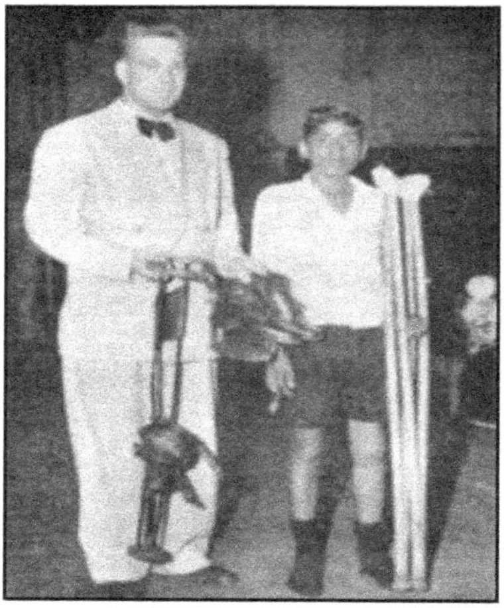

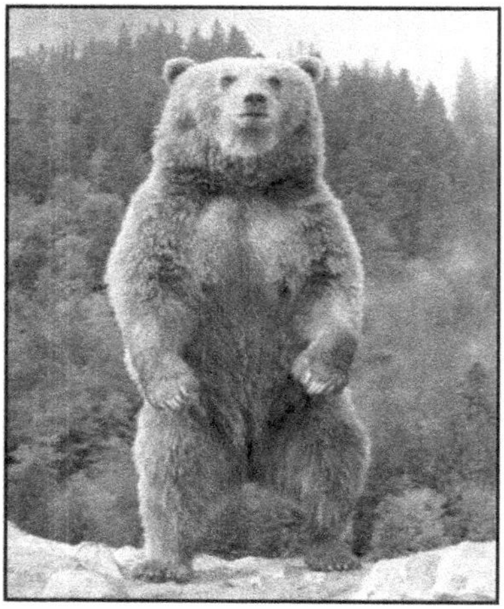

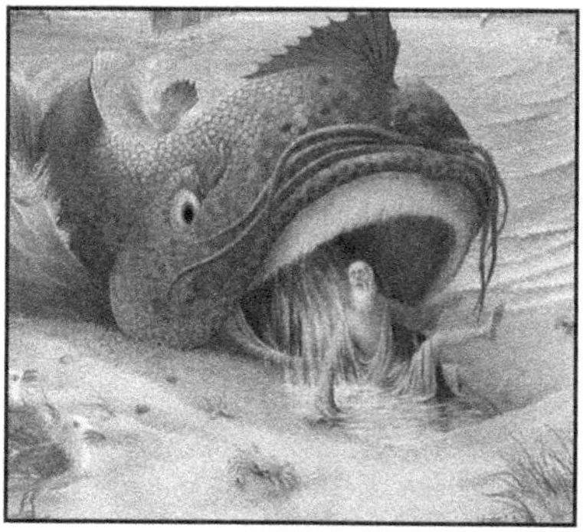

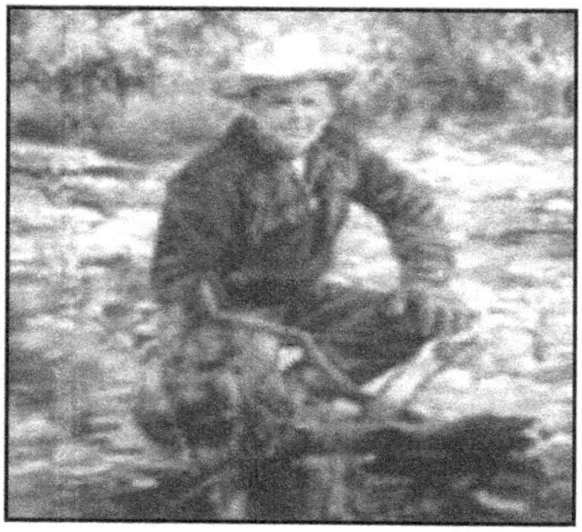

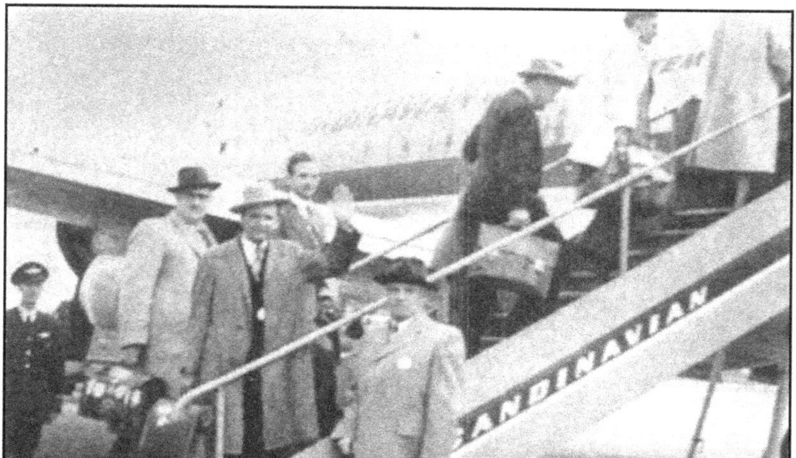
ANDINAVIAN

CHAPTER ONE
A SEARCH FOR SCRIPTURAL AND PROPHETIC TRUTH

Thomas Albert, a man in his young fifties, being well dressed, was stepping up the stairs of Salem, Oregon's Talk Show studio building and paused to face the camera. "Won't you join me in a search for the truth of the life and times of a most phenomenal character of modern times? We start our in-depth study inside."

Stepping into the studio room Tom walked over to a large world globe and placed his finger on the little country of Israel. As he slowly rotated the globe he explained: "The Sages and Prophets tell us that the sun that rises in the east is the same sun which sets in the west. Let's go some one hundred and eighty degrees."

The globe then stopped, and the camera zoomed in on Tucson, Arizona. (An analogy of the S-O-N arriving in the United States). Thomas walked over to sit at the table where he hosted today's confrontational subject with two gentlemen wearing a jacket, tie and a strained smile.

"Gentlemen, I thank you both for coming out to this evening's show. For this is a topic that is a tough one, the legendary figure of William Branham."

Thomas turned towards the camera: "Ladies and gentlemen, please welcome our guests today. We have here, Doctor PEARY GREEN, he is a graduate from

Southwestern Bible Institute and, also, a writer of several books, and a well- known apologist. Incidentally, it was Billy Paul Branham, son of Mr. Branham who attended the same college. That was short term, I believe?"

Dr. Peary answered, "Yes, introductions and close association were initiated there." Thomas said, "Also, we have here with us Historian, Author and longtime Evangelist/Teacher, Jeremy Revelatee. Let's give them a hand."

An applause from the studio guests went up. Thomas faced the table.

"Gentlemen, we seek the truth regarding an Evangelist with tremendous success of a healing deliverance ministry, Reverend William Branham. Let me give a brief background for the audience's sake. His birth was in a Kentucky log cabin, to a very poor Charles and Ella Branham. This character caused a great stir, swept the world, for both good and bad. An amber light whirled into the room on April the 6th, 1909 upon his birth and hoovered over the infant. Later, him having entered the ministry as a twenty-one-year-old, many supernatural phenomena had taken place. WILLIAM BRANHAM is the subject today, whether or not he is a man to be reckoned with, in terms of legitimacy, theology, and the twentieth century Prophet, as some allude. What really happened to him. Doctor Peary?"

Doctor Peary shrugged slightly, exhaled through his nose and put on a smile. "I must say, the man was very bold. However, the main-stream Council of Theologians consider him far reaching in his assumptions of qualifications. His spiritual mentors and sponsors are nigh unto non-existent."

Silence was heavy in the pause.

Professor Jeremy spoke up, "The first pitch hit out of the park, there." Gratefully, everyone laughed.

"However, while some may react with similar disregard to him based strictly from the perspective of a linguist or theologian, comparing diphthongs or the like; his ministry set a new pinnacle, for his overall results in helping humanity and the validation of a supernatural God."

Thomas spoke, "Is it possible that he would intentionally set himself up, the stage around him... (through my brief research) he often used word phrases, and allegory, where others might think him a, as a...?"

Professor Jeremy, "As a Fop?" Thomas retorted, "exactly." The Professor added, "Yes, I believe..."

Dr. Peary stepped in to say, "I don't believe that is the case with this BRENNEN."

Jeremy responded, "You are referring to Branham, William Branham, after his names sake, the Prophet Abraham."

Doctor Peary, "Yes, he simply flounders around in vocabulary trying to find the appropriate words, from a sixth-grade education, in hopes of befuddling the young and weaker minds."

Professor Jeremy, "May I inject? An actor may play many parts by wearing a mask to portray another role, yet is he not the same person behind the mask all the time? He slams his education, his nature, spouts that he's a man with issues. William Branham continually throws himself under the bus, (so to speak) wearing only a mask or facade, to stay hidden. A sinful-natured man does not discern the secrets of other men's hearts and lives, such as did the Lord Jesus."

Doctor Peary disturbed, answered, "He uses, 'Thus saith the Lord,' as a manipulative tool to stop any opposition, while interpreting the scripture to suit his position at the moment."

Professor Jeremy, "William Branham has made clear that actions speak louder to God than do our words. A person may bring dialogue as to give a persona without presenting his true character. The paradox via...shall we say, 'camouflage'?"

The room seemed to pause to catch its breath. Thomas spoke, "Perhaps, he just had the ability to keep his ear attuned to the symphony and an eye on the Conductor, rather than be drawn to the praises of the audience. "

Professor Jeremy, "touché, just so."

Thomas turned toward the camera and smiled, "I'm sorry to say our time is up and perhaps if it is agreeable with the both of you (he turned his head slightly to the guest speakers) we could use this subject matter, though barely touched, as an introduction to a series."

Both gentlemen agreed with a nod. (Turning back to the camera) "We now leave you to ponder on, pro and con, was William Branham Prophet or Pope, friend or foe, maybe even a secret coming of the Messiah? Who was William Branham? Until next time, keep the faith and a smile."

Thomas stepped away from the studio and made his way to a coffee pot to refill his cup. Jeremy joined him. Thomas spoke in low tones, "You really think that there is more than what first meets the eye…, referring to Mr. Branham?"

Professor Jeremy, "Absolutely, without doubt. There are far too many instances where his life exposes Jesus Christ alive again, and him disguising the evidence. It is apparent, to him the seals are open, yet, he says that the trumpets or thunders hold the end time truths. His life is paradoxical."

Thomas answered back, "We ought to go further. A deeper investigation is in order. Perhaps, I should have resorted to teaching a dissecting class to college grads." Thomas raised a quizzical brow.

The aged scholar patted him on the shoulder. Jeremy, "Very good, my boy. And keep in mind that this is not merely a search for historical facts upon facts; the end-time Messiah will be as always, hidden from the obvious. It's a puzzle for splicing or the placing of hundreds of pieces, 'til it makes the picture...You can't merely, 'push play.'"

SWEETWATER, TENNESSEE
THOMAS ALBERT RESIDENCE

Thomas sat up in bed with a laptop computer on his lap. He scrolled down to the end-time message of William Branham and went to the "Table" icon.

CHAPTER TWO
CHILDHOOD - A DIFFICULT LIFE

JEFFERSONVILLE, INDIANA
OLD HOME STEAD – DIRT PATH TO THE CREEK

Billy (seven years old) struggled as he lifted two large buckets from the nearby creek and hurried along the trail. One, then two hundred yards but that's all he could go; he needed a rest stop. As he sat down on an old log, he noticed a cocoon move just up from where placed his hand. On closer observation he laid down on the grass to watch this wonder. With a few struggles, the worm emerged.

"Why? It's not a worm, not now, anyhow?" Billy exclaimed.

The butterfly pulled itself from a wad, now freed from its would-be coffin. It stretched out its wings slowly.

"Wow, he's beautiful."

Billy jumped up and hustled down the path. First there was the sound of a thud, a stumble, then buckets sloshed, and water splashed out.

"Ooouh, Yoouch! Louzy no good root. Ooh, ooh it gashed my toe open." Billy slowly picked himself up and tied an old cob under his bleeding toe. He then carried what little water he had left, and with no-one else with him, he limped along, toe still throbbing. As he walked, he passed beneath a large sycamore tree and he came to a sudden stop. "What is that?" He said with surprise. There under the sycamore tree a small whirlwind started spinning right directly in front of him. "What? What is this?" Billy said to himself. Just then he heard a strange voice who spoke from out of the whirlwind.

"You are not to smoke, or drink, or defile your body with women, for I have a work for you to do when you are older," said the voice.

To this seven-year-old, a whirlwind that spoke with a voice like a man was creepy and just way too much. Billy threw up his arms and sent the buckets and water flying in the air. His screams rang out through that old dirt path... frightful screams. You can hear the patter of his bare feet running along the pathway toward home, as fast as his legs could take him.

FOUR YEARS HAVE PASSED

Now, 11-year-old Billy is walking the wooded path with a little school friend named Emma, they both go this direction to their homes after school. It was quiet as they walked the path through the woods, all except for a few birds in the trees chirping their songs. Neither one talked a word though – they tried to think of something to talk about, but Billy was a quiet shy boy, and it was hard for him to get the courage inside himself, but he finally did, he mustered up the words to say, "I, umm... I'll ... May I carry your books for you?"

Today was especially hard for Billy, he was humbled and embarrassed by such shabby clothes he had to wear that day. On this day, although it was a balmy warm afternoon, he kept a woolen coat on throughout the whole day. Suddenly, like out of nowhere, six loud irate boys ran up and started circling around them both.

"So, there you are Emma." "Ma's gonna be really mad if you are late getting home," sharply snapped one of the boys to Emma.

"Sides, what you doing hanging around with the likes of him?," said the other boy.

"Ya, what I hear, his Pa's the town drunk and...and also, this here trash stinks like wood smoke, of skinned critters and who knows what all," snarked a third boy.

This whole time the boys got Billy away from Emma and formed a tight circle around him and started pushing him back and forth. Billy trying to be brave, the schoolbooks went flying out from Billy's grasp.

"Say, ain't those Emma's books you got there? Who do you think your walking with? She's, my girlfriend," shouted a boy from the group.

Their pushing continued so roughly until Billy's woolen coat tore open revealing that he was without a shirt under his coat. Their laughter roared as all six boys started mocking and pushing him even more, then they jerked his coat off of him which threw Billy to the ground. The six boys showed no mercy as they began kicking Billy again and again until blood was running from his nose and mouth.

Moaning Billy cried, "Please, please! Ok, ok! I'll go! I'll go straight home. I meant no harm. Wanted to be part... of...some friends." As he gasped for a breath.

"Friends? You'll never have friends," snapped a boy. Billy broke away and took off running harder than he had ever ran before, racing through the familiar path of the woods back to his house. Up the front porch he ran and to the door which stood open and just inside the door he swiftly reached up to grab his .22 rifle, taking it down from its resting place. Running swiftly back down the old path to where the boys had beat him, he found the six boys there, still in the same place. Without hesitation Billy stopped and stood in the middle of the pathway pointing his rifle in their direction. Each of the boys stared at the rifle in Billy's hand and his fierce anger as he stared them down with blood still dripping from the cuts on his eye and mouth.

Billy growled the words; "Which one of you wants it first, so you won't have to watch the others die." Billy, with his crack-shot skills was sure to get them all before they could escape. The woods quickly rang with screaming and stomping of many feet as the boys ran as fast and as far into the woods as they could in every direction. Snapping and ratcheting of the lever action carbine was the only other sounds heard for the first few seconds, as every shell would not fire. He quickly reloaded the shells, and you could hear the echoes in the woods of the rapid rifle fire, as all sixteen bullets let loose into a nearby dead snag. Moments later it all settled, and the quiet peacefulness of the woods returned. Billy hung his head down low, dropped to his knees in exhaustion, pain and anguish and started half crying and half laughing in rage.

"Town drunk...they don't...thrown out..." Billy sobbed again. "I just wanted friends."

TWO YEARS LATER
(Ext. Louisville Kentucky Fairgrounds Night)

Billy, fifteen years old, and his cousin, along with a friend Jimmy Poole, were walking along checking out all the exhibits and games, when William spotted a shooting gallery booth, and wanted to show off some skills.

"Hey Jimmy, how much money you got?," says Billy. "I got fifteen cents and can win something nice, if we go in together," Jimmy answered.

As the boys were walking away from the shooting booth, Jimmy exclaimed, "You sure showed d'm folks what's it all about. Let me see that knife you won."

The boys were strolling along when a young lady's voice caught their attention. Sitting beside her tent-booth, was an attractive Gypsy girl calling to them.

"Hey there, you with the stripped cardigan on. Yes you, come here," the girl said as she was looking at Billy.

The boys, both intrigued and surprised by this charmer, made their way over to her. Jimmy spoke up, "Howdy Ma'am, was you speaking to us there?"

"Well, yes... more specifically to this young fellow here," looking at Billy, "Did you know that a light follows you? You were born unto a divine purpose, by a specific sign."

Billy was startled, "Look lady, quiet on that stuff. I got...I got to go. Let's git," Billy quickly says to Jimmy.

William quickly bumps his hasty retreat through the boys. They look at the gypsy girl with a quizzical face, shrug their shoulders and hustle to catch up.

After Jimmy caught up with Billy, he quizzically asks, "What was that all about?"

Billy shrugged, "Nothing, Ma says them folks ain't no count. She says, that dem folks are of no never mind, that they're of the devil."

FIVE YEARS LATER

Billy, now sixteen, and Jimmy Poole are in their neighbor's father's Ford coupe, making plans on taking a couple girls out for a soda and sandwiches. Jimmy popped up with, "What you driving like a slug for when girls are awaiting? Let's get..."

Billy was driving along Urban area and pulled up to the girls. The girls got in and the drive continued.

Hope, Billy's girlfriend said, "You get out like this much, Billy?" To which Billy replied, "Not too often, cause I'm mostly busy. I got big plans you know; I plan on going pro in the big ring matches." He looked green and red around the gills. He was having a great time feeling important and trying to keep pace with the other boy's stories. He cleared his throat. He stopped at a scenic look out where there was another young couple waiting. His girl got out of the car and opened her small purse and lit-up a cigarette. Hope asked, "Want a cigarette, Billy?" "What," he responds, "No Ma'am, I don't smoke." Hope shook her head and said, "Now what? You don't smoke, you say you don't dance, and you don't go to theaters. What do you do?" His response was a little shaken. "I go fishing, hunting... mostly." Hope said, "Here have a cigarette." "No, thank you, just the same," Billy responded.

The rest of the group were interested by this time and stepped over to listen in.

Hope put her hand on her hip after taking the cigarette back out her mouth. "You big sissy!" The group closed in and started sneering. Billy snapped up the cigarette. "Give me that cigarette, I'll show you whether I'm a sissy or not." Billy grabbed the cigarette and one of the other boys handed him a lighter. He started to light it when he began to hear the sound of a wind blowing. The experience of the whirling-wind in the tree, from years ago, gripped him. The Angel's voice repeated in his head, "Don't you never...." Billy quickly threw the cigarette down and ran away. The laughter and jeers from the group fiercely bit him as he tried to outrun them.

EXT. JEFFERSONVILLE CITY TRANSIT BUS

The bus surged forward. William, now around seventeen years old, was wearing his Game-Warden uniform. He stepped into the bus and made his way to the upper handrail and grabbed hold. Across the aisle was a stout looking, very nicely dressed lady. She was looking at him.

"How do you do? I'm Mrs. Davenport." Billy looked her way but only held eye contact but for a second. Billy's response was short. "Good afternoon."

Mrs. Davenport spoke confidently, "You're lonesome, aren't you?"

Billy said, "No ma'am."

"Well, you're not at home," she inserted, "You were born to be out in the west. Isn't that correct?"

Billy, "Say? What are you taking about?"

Mrs. Davenport said, "I better explain myself. You see, I'm an Astrologist. I would like to speak with you for just a minute, if I may?" With his head turned, Billy acted as if he didn't hear her. She continued, "I just wondered if you knew that you were born under a star, a specific sign?"

Billy was taken back and blurted, "Look lady, I don't want to know nothing more about that. I don't mean to be ungentlemanly, but I ain't religious or nothing." Mrs. Davenport, "I am not speaking of religion. Well, ...would it help if I could tell you exactly when you were born? Would that help prove to you?"

Billy responded with, "Firstly, you couldn't do that."

"Oh, but I can," said Mrs. Davenport, "It was April the 6th at five o'clock in the morning, 1909." Billy stared at her a minute then turned his head.

CHAPTER THREE
GOING OUT WEST - SEEKING HIS DESTINY

EXT. ARIZONA
WESTERN CLOTHING AND TACK STORE

Billy turned his head towards his cowboy partner. They were outside a country tack store looking at a poster hung up in the window. Their clothes were tattered.

"Hey, listen to this. They're giving prize money to winners of the nine different rodeo events. If I'm to do this right, I Recon' I'll need to go in and get me some gear and duds." Billy was trying on some flashy chaps over a pair of new Levi's. The big chaps had a skull of a Texas Longhorn bull on them. Billy's cowboy partner gave out a guff, "Now, you'd be the ace #1 cowpoke for sure, with them chaps... if'n, there wasn't eighteen inches of dem' still laying on the ground." They both broke-up in laughter. Billy admitted, "Ya, sorta looks like one of them Bantam roosters...feathers all down over his feet."

EXT. ARIZONA CATTLE RANCH – DAY

The ranch boss rode out onto the back pastureland on his buckskin stallion and spotted Billy riding fence. He galloped down the slope and met up with his new hired hand. Hector called out to Billy, "Ho, there Bill." Billy stopped, tipped his hat and threw a knee over the saddle horn for a minute of saddle rest.

"Morning Boss, Morning to you, what's left of it." Hector was quieting his horse down from a good run, by patting its neck. "Wow there, everything ferrying good?" Billy replied, "There was a stretch of wire out towards Harry's place that could use tightening, before they start pushing through it."

It is obvious Hector was in a hurry and spun his horse around. "We'll get some boys on it in the morning. We will be pushing five hundred head of that new Hereford breed, down here come next week. Keep an eye out for a couple wet cows or calves, they been missing – out in the sage probably. Oh, there is a killer bull that broke into the ranch recently and would love to catch you in an arroyo or box canyon." Billy slipped his leg off and stepped back into the stirrup. "Right..."

Hector jerked his steed and started to ride back but then pulled up again, "I forgot to give you this letter." Billy swung his mount alongside. "Thank you, see you this afternoon." Billy opened the letter with a tremor of anticipation. As the lines are read His face dropped and his throat filled. With a mournful stare, he looked east towards home. "Got to get back. Got to go home."

CHAPTER FOUR
SURRENDER TO CHRIST - A CALL TO THE MINISTRY
INT. JEFFERSONVILLE PENTECOSTAL BAPTIST CHURCH – 1932

William Branham was sitting in the rear pew and noticed Hope Brumback sitting further up. Pastor Davis dismissed the church meeting, and they all stood up to leave. William stood with his western hat in hand, then decided to step out. William started to head for the sidewalk. Hope called out, "Bill, Bill" William stopped and turned. Hope moved through the crowd and approached. "Hey there, Miss Hope," William said. Hope answered back, "Where you been keeping yourself?" William responded, "Arizona... cowboy-un. See ya are going to church now. If you are heading home, mind if we walk together?" The two walked alone but had a difficult time starting conversation. Hope, "Bill, why did you leave without a word?"

William answered, "Seemed apparent that you were looking for some other type of person than myself..., to me anyway."

Hope, "Shameful, wasn't I. How can I ever make amends? Really, it wasn't that way at all, I missed you immediately. I couldn't focus, my work and other activities, other relationships were empty, just... a shambles." William said, "I wasn't much of a cowpoke either. Once we stopped at a Dude store to get some duds for the rodeo, and the chaps

I tried on were hanging eighteen inches on the ground." They looked at each other and blurted out laughing. They stop walking and turned toward each other and touched hands. They walked again with her head on his shoulder.

EXT. LOUISVILLE, INDIANA
OHIO RIVER SIDE – 1933

A bright July afternoon was filled with ruckus, as people moved up and down the riverbank during a baptismal service. A dark-haired minister (24 years old) that was short, almost frail and nearly illiterate was officiating it. William asked Hope to read the text for baptism.

William, "I know, but I can't…don't read so good. You just be a darling and read the text for… ok? I love you."

William patted her arm as he headed out into the river. She turned the bible open as he stepped towards the water. Hope turned to the gathering and spoke up, "The Holy Scriptures state…go ye out to the whole world baptizing in the name of the Father, Son and Holy Ghost…"

William slipped off his loafers and stepped into the water and began baptizing. The seventeenth repentant approached for their turn, when just then a startling amber light descended from the heavens over the group. Many who attended fainted from the experience. William Branham was shocked at the sight of a whirling ball of fire which came near and hovered just above his head. An Angelic voice spoke out, "As John the Baptizer, fore-ran my first coming, so shall you fore-run my second coming."

The crowd was filled with expectation as William struggled to get a grip on his emotions after the experience and then continued the baptism.

William spoke, "As I baptize you with water for the repentance of sin in Jesus Christ's name, so too, may He baptize you with the Holy Ghost for regeneration."

EXT. JEFFERSONVILLE STREET
COURIER NEWS BUILDING – EARLY MORNING
(Indiana records of marriage license and Billy Paul's birth date)

Paper boys scattered in every direction with the mornings latest from the Courier Journal.

Paper boy, "Read all about it, a mystic light is seen over young minister's head. Extra, extra, read all about it."

Hope Brumback and William stepped out of church and started walking home from the meeting. William said, "Did you get my letter?" Hope, "Um-hum" William, "Did you read it?" William glanced over to her in apprehension. Hope, "Um-hum. I love you too Billy, but I must tell you something before any more..." She coughed out a cry. "Shameful. I went to a party some months back and a guy got me a drink; one led to a second, then another. Before I knew it, I was beguiled by him. I am... three months pregnant. Nobody knows but you." They stopped walking and turned towards each other. She was tearful.

William dipped his head a moment before answering, "I see." A pause. William cleared his throat, "I still will care for you. I'll still marry you. It does not change my feelings toward you. We must not delay but get to a preacher right away. You're too nice a person to let this get out."

EXT. FORT WAYNE, INDIANA – CHURCH DAY

The newlyweds had rice tossed over them as they made their get-away from the wedding ceremony. Their feet were seen walking away while laughter was heard.

INT. JEFFERSONVILLE – OFFICE OF DR. DAVIS

William's step was a little halted approaching the door with the name plate, "Missionary Pentecostal/Baptist Church, Pastor office." He went through the door bashfully for he was unprepared and was dressed rather humbly. Two distinguished gentlemen were there who greeted William rather coolly and began to question him. The office was plush, decorated lavishly with a huge custom-made oak desk. There was a Persian rug in the middle of the hardwood floor. The Assistant Pastor started in, "Won't you sit down. So, how do these trances come upon you? When do they happen, here in the church auditorium?"

William Branham said, "Not so much, just mostly any time...when in prayer. They're...I don't know...not dreams, more like movies or trances. I see things take place."

Doctor Davis folded his hands over his pompous chest. "I see. I'm glad you came in and shared this with us, because these kinds of spiritual things are the dabbling with the occult or what is called spiritualism."

The grilling faded from William's hearing as he turned to the window and the view changed.

VISION BEGINS. 1937 FLOOD.

Just then a vision broke before his eyes. He was witnessing a tyrannical rainstorm. A storm of rising waters, dikes and levy's bulging as waters reached their tops and poured over; the dikes gave way and the twenty-mile-wide valley was flooded. Houses and buildings were toppled. There was a massive death toll, and a terrible cry of anguish went out. He stared with his mouth open. A man in a boat measured the flood waters at twenty-two feet deep.

VISION ENDS.

Doctor Davis' voice faded in. William shook his head a bit and blinked. "You remember how King Saul was backslid, speaking to the Witch of Endor."

INT. THE FISH AND GAME DEPT. LUNCH HALL FEBRUARY 1937

A score of uniformed gents (along with Bill Branham) of the Rangers Station were hurrying to take a place at the long mess hall table and benches.

William looked over to the captain and coughed, "sir." His apprehension to approach him was noticed. They all noticed it because they remembered other times where William Branham had spoken of a dream or vision that he had recently had. He continued, "has there been any reports of a heavy storm heading this way?" The captain glanced over and said, "not to my knowledge. Why?" William cleared his throat, "I was in a minister's meeting with Pastor Davis, and I looked out the window and saw a vision of a terrible storm where all the levees and bridges broke, houses collapsed, and people drowned. Someone measured the water depth in the street to be twenty-three feet deep." The captain looked a bit pale, but William was glad he spoke it out.

The crew leader of number six spoke up, "Oh really, so how about telling us another one of the stories that are a little more believable, like maybe a twelve-foot bear swallows a cowboy whole... Stetson, boots-n-spurs included."

He looked at William. A roar of Laughter went up. He pointed William to a bulletin board to see a Jeffersonville newspaper clipping, which stated it's historical all time flood depth of eighteen inches. William in frustration, hurriedly left the table and went out the door.

EXT. FOREST, INDIANA – JANUARY

Out in the woods in his uniform and with his gun on his hip, William was in his domain. His eyes scanned out into the wooded cathedral. Sunbeams caused the icicles to appear seven colors, like a prism. A black-tailed buck stepped out along the pathway, not twenty yards off. William ran his hands across the needles of a pine. He took in a deep breath and opened his arms and spun around and laughed. A hare hopped out onto a patch of snow near his feet, to eat some clover.

INDIANA WEATHER RADIO CHANNEL
THREE MONTHS LATER
(Notes from Sermon, 1951 Life Story)

Air ways are pumping out a news flash of flood warnings for all of Clark counties and the Louisville areas. Rain, snow and sleet pounded for twelve days straight. The temperature began to drop. Radio news flashes were on every station, giving out warnings. At a well-liked pub and diner, a group of people stopped their discussions, eating and drinking, and moved over to the radio for updates and road closures.

"Death toll is now up to 320 with much more expected. We will have updates of casualties coming in throughout lower Indiana counties and upper Kentucky, that is, as long as the power poles remain standing.

Flood waters have reached an all-time high, exceeding the flood of 1913. Stay away from all dams and levees, as authorities are now preparing for them to give-way."

William in his uniform was frantically piloting his aluminum skiff through the streets and alleyways flooded by the rising waters. A house crumbled and was swept away. He quieted the motor at times to hear the cries of those that were now desperately stranded on roof tops. A lady cried out for help, "Here, over here. Over here, please, over here."

William quickly motored over there and saw a lady and three children clinging to a chimney, shivering and crying. A siren was blaring away. Rushing water was taking homes and vehicles in its torrent.

The stranded lady in gratitude said, "Thank God for you, thank you, thank you." William maneuvered the little dingy around to lean close to the chimney. "I got you, ok, you're safe now. It's all going to be ok. Ma'am, let the littlest one come in first. Step in the middle of the boat, don't walk around. Set down quickly. In the middle son, in the middle, yes. Now you, Ma'am."

William hurried across the river to the Louisville side. The assistant game warden was waiting for him to arrive. He tied his boat up to a guardrail and helped with the children.

The Assistant Warden clasped William's hand warmly, "Bill, glad you made it. Chief wanted me to tell you that they have been putting everyone on rail cars and bringing them here to Louisville. Your wife and kids are here now. I got word that she is very sick and is calling for you."

The lady which was just let out of the boat shouted, "oh My baby, oh my baby. Oh God."

William looked her way, thinking that they had left another child back at the house, he turned quickly and jumped for the boat. "I'll hurry back and...."

William zoomed off without looking back. He reached for the house with water now up above the roof line and the water tearing it apart. William kept the engine running. He tied the boat to an antenna standing up high and scrambled through the attic hatch door. He is gone only a moment and then returned empty handed without any child or infant. The hatch was now taking in water fast and he waded through now knee-deep water back to reach the boat when the chimney broke off. The house shifted and crumbled as William jumped for the boats rope line. The boat tipped up just as the rope was released. William crawled into the craft. He cranked up the boats throttle. Halfway across the now swelled river with three-foot waves, the motor sputtered, then coughed into silence. He pulled on the starting cord several times without success. He adjusted the choke knob, and his eyes shifted, he can hear the Ohio river waterfalls somewhere in the distance. Sweat and fatigue were written all over his face.

William called on God, "Oh, dear Lord, my helper."

The killer falls now can be heard roaring just yards away and darkness of night had closed in. "Come to my aide, oh Lord. I am in need of you. Why didn't they listen to me?" The engine caught and William gave it all he had. The little boat could hardly make any headway because of the tremendous current. He slowly pulled away from the brink of the falls and spotted a shadow of a small island where he beached the boat. William was alone in the dark and huddled down, head on knees, crying. The swirling water spun in his mind as he faded off into a fitful slumber.

FLOODED OHIO RIVER ISLAND
TWO DAYS LATER – MORNING

William stood by the edge of the island and looked out upon the floating rubble. The waters had abated some. He climbed into the boat and grabbed the engine pull cord and started across.

LOUISVILLE SCHOOL GYMNASIUM DAY

Hundreds of flood patients were on stretchers or just blankets, upon the floor. Nurses were attending the suffering. Someone was mopping up the blood from the new arrivals. William was frantically searching among the suffering and tearful loved ones. Desperately he called out, "Hope...Hope where are you? Hope, can you hear me?"

Looking about, he saw a hand raise up from a cot placed far back in a corner. He had to step over and around hundreds of flood patients to get to her. He reached out for her hand that was near to limp. By her side he knelt and took her frail hand. She was pale and her voice was weak. William tried to grasp the seriousness of her health. "Hope honey, I'm so sorry. I had no Idea. Never again, will I...of course you're going to be alright." Hope whispered a reply, "Bill, you're here. Why did you call me back, honey?"

William patted her hand and said, "Back... back from where?"

Hope, "Remember telling me of that wonderful land just beyond. You called me from there. I was there, Bill. I saw it all and it is far more wonderful than any description." A pause, William started to tremble.

Hope, "You do know why this is happening, don't you? When mother called them Holiness people, trash...we never should've listened to her. You don't need people's approval, acceptance...they don't understand."

William responded, "Yes dear, that's right. But Billy Paul and baby girl, they need you...I need you. Why talk like this?"

Hope shook her head and smiled weakly, "It's ok Bill, I have to go back now, but promise me that you'll not stay alone, they'll need a mother. Meda loves you and I'm sure she will be of great help. I'm going now Bill." Hope looked up and his face slowly faded out.

William saw her depart and he called out, "Hope honey, I will gather the kiddies and we'll meet at the Eastern gate. Look for me, I will be calling your name."

CHAPTER FIVE
THE WEEPING PROPHET

JEFFERSONVILLE
FISH AND GAME OFFICE
TWO DAYS LATER

William stepped into the office, took off his gun belt and placed it on the counter. The Warden Stevens stepped out of his office, "Hey, Bill come here a minute, will you." Stevens got up from his chair just as William came into the room. He placed his hand on William's shoulder. "Bill, I want you to take a few days off, to be with your family... the children. You know what I mean. I'm so sorry for you Bill, what happened."

William says, "Can't Boss…can't. I just got to keep busy. So many people at loss or injured. I'll be fine."

The phone rang in next office. A fellow officer answered the phone, and they could hear him say, "Fish and Game dept... Bill, it's for you."

William stepped out of Warden's office and grabbed hold of the phone. He looked crushed. Doctor Sam Adair was heard on the other line, "Bill…ah…Bill, you better come in right away, it's little Sharon…Bill." The silence was all that one could hear. Sam Adair, "She's dying! She contacted it from her mother."

LOUISVILLE HOSPITAL DAY

William was speaking to the Doctor and nurse in the hallway.

Doctor Sam spoke to William, "Now Bill, you just can't go to her, you will spread it to Billy Paul if you do. She'll be gone in a few minutes. Here, sit down here. Take this relaxant that the nurse has for you, it'll help you with all this upset, some."

William said, "I just got to see her. Where...are they holding her, Doc?"

Doctor Sam, "Now Billy, you know that's impossible. You got to think of your boy. We have her in the basement room."

The nurse handed him the pills and water. He put the pills in his mouth and took the water. The doctor grabbed his arm.

Doctor says, "We'll get through this. Need me for anything, I'll be near." The Nurse and doctor left. William stood up and spit the sedatives out into planter then went through the door heading for the staircase. The little eight-month-old baby screamed out and was in convulsions. William stood over her trembling.

William called to her, "Daddy's little darling, I love you so much. You are so precious to me...Daddy is going to take you home real soon now."

William took her hand that was shaking terribly. "Oh, great God of heaven and earth look down upon this baby child and magnify your name. Get glory...Oh Lord, hear my prayer and set her free from this pestilence."

Baby Sharon squealed in such pain – her eyes crossed. Her little mouth came open...she was going.

Satan spoke to William mockingly, "thought he was a God of love. He doesn't love you. He doesn't care for you, nor for yours."

William took a deep breath, "The Lord gives and takes, blessed be the name of the Lord. You know daddy, honey? God bless you, darling. You're an Angel. You're going to be with Mama now." "Lord, you know I've done wrong. But, as Job-of-old said, 'though you slay me, yet I trust you.'" Take her if it's your will, Lord. Little One, I will lay you on mommy's bosom." He cried great sobs as his little girl left the world.

JEFFERSONVILLE, INDIANA – CEMETERY

William and young Billy Paul were weeping as they made their way slowly up a small grassy slope of the cemetery. Their polished black shoes stepping on the turf were the only things you could hear on that crisp morning. A child and a man were seen walking up and stopped just before a grave site with the names of Hope and Sharon Rose Branham on it.

PUBLIC ELECTRIC POWER – TWO WEEKS LATER

William was splicing primary power wires at the top of a pole to restore electricity. He was standing in his spurs and pole belt. His tears flowing, but he tried to work. William began to sing brokenly, "on a hill far away stood an...an old rugged cross."

William looked out to another pole, and he saw the sign of the cross, with Jesus hanging on it. "Yes, it was my sins that put Him on there. I was the one who nailed Him to the cross, the Prince of life. But, oh God, somewhere in heaven, you got my little girl..." He saw her again struggling in pain. He saw his little girl's last few horrendous suffering moments. William's face crumbled. He took off his rubber gloves and in despair he said, "Sharry honey, Daddy's coming to see you this morning."

He grabbed the wire. He then found himself slumped over at the base of the pole. His clothes were smoking. He got his wits about him and released the climber's belt and staggered to his truck. He stepped into his house tattered and broken but unable to settle down. He was seen stomping back and forth in his house alone, struggling to control his emotions. He grabbed his head and pulled his hair, and he let out a huge bellow – tears streaming down his face.

William cried out, "I just can't take this...I'm losing my mind. No, no I just can't...I'll go as a quitter before I bring an approach to Christ, of insanity."

Stepping to the counter, he took out a wooden locker and threw it open. Reaching in he pulled out his thirty-eight and loaded six rounds, quickly. Kneeling beside the bed, he prayed as he put the gun to his head, "And forgive us our trespasses and sins as we..." The trigger is squeezed tightly but it is stuck in place. He threw the gun against the wall, which then fired.

THE OLD BRANHAM HOMESTEAD HOUSE – 1938

The screen door slammed behind Mom Branham as she quickly jerked off her apron. She turned back to look out the door as William walked up towards the house. He approached the weathered door, the screen half torn off. Both William and his mother looked tired and worn. William staggered up the old steps and opened the screen door and called out, "Ma?"

His mother came into the room, "Oh Bill, Bill you look a sight." William explained, "Hate to impose on you Ma but..., well, I just couldn't stay in the house and..." His mother said, "Ain't no thing son, know that. You just stay as long as you need. Billy Paul is at your sister's, I recon...?" William responded, "Yes, he's there all right for few."

Mom Branham, "Now, don't you worry about a thing. Got your old room all ready, you can just move your things in."

William says, "No Mom, no need for that...we'll be fine...we'll just stay in the little houseboat for a while."

Mom Branham said, "well ok, now you stop with all that, just relax here, rest."

William, "Thanks Mom for inviting me...the house... with all the mem..." She waves and pats him on the shoulder.

JEFFERSONVILLE-OLD HOME STEAD
FOUR MONTHS LATER

William heard a knock and went to open the door for Meda, who was seventeen years old now – William let her in through the door.

William smiled as he greeted the young lady, "Hello there Meda, please come in. MOTHER, I want to introduce you to one of Hope's friends, Meda." Mom Branham was sitting in an easy chair and Meda stepped over to her.

Mom Branham, "Child, you seem quite young, but bright."

Meda responded, "Thank you Ma'am, I am now seventeen and have baby-sat the neighbor's children since I was eleven."

William conjectured, "She comes with good credentials and is of noble stock." William smiled at her and Meda was glad for the support.

JEFFERSONVILLE – OFFICE OF DR. DAVIS
ONE YEAR LATER

As William Branham stepped through the door, he saw a large group of ministers already seated and staring at him, as he gently shut the door.

Dr. Davis greeted William while he stepped to the long table. "We are discussing the subject of our appearance in the public eye, our image and the future perspective of society, the governments."

William was noticeably taken-back by this. This approach, and main concern of men of God, the community's spiritual leaders, repulsed him. William spoke back, "I thought our responsibility was to God firstly, to give the community a concise biblical view of God's will."

Dr. Davis, "Yes, it is Billy, but we are getting off the issue of why we called you into the office. What's this I hear about Angels or these voices that are supposed to be speaking to you?"

The Assistant Pastor got up and paced about the room, making it obvious that he was irritated. He said, "That is not all, they have printed out in the Journal that a mysterious light came out from the heavens and scared the bunch of you, while baptizing at the river. We are being rumored about as radical and soon they shall claim our congregation is rolling in the aisles."

Dr. Davis, "That's about enough of this super-duper spiritualism, young man. We'll have no more of these…

these escapades. The church board will most likely recommend a probationary period, if you persist."

JEFFERSONVILLE – OFFICE OF DR. DAVIS
SOME MONTHS LATER

Pastor Davis was sitting in his high-backed leather chair at the end of the table. Several members of the of the Ministerial Board of directors were at the table and the Assistant Pastor was standing at the window. William entered the room and stood somewhat apprehensive with his hat in hand.

William Branham approached and spoke quickly. He remained standing. "If it please the board, I would like to be excused from the meeting." The First Member spoke up, "All meetings with the agenda that we face today are mandatory in attendance."

The Assistant Pastor, still with his back turned spun around sharply. "Mandatory indeed, for we are needing to confront certain behaviors."

William said, "May I ask a question regarding doctrine of the church?"

Dr. Davis replied, "It is of utmost urgency that the matter-at-hand be dealt with this morning but let us allow for this concern of our fellow elder."

William planned his words carefully, "Thank you, for the audience. My question that is puzzling me is, does the Baptist Church advocate the ordination of women preachers? For I was in study and read in Corinthians how they must remain silent in the church."

The table erupted in much clamor and disagreements. The Assistant Pastor turned towards the group.

Assistant Pastor, "Please gentlemen, please. It is evidently a matter which will take considerably more time then we have at present time. Now, let us return to the matter of the compliance to the church."

Second Member spoke in curt tones, "Pastor, I believe that this is the third time you have had him in the office on these matters. I am referring to Branham."

Assistant Pastor, "Shall we cut to the chase, gentlemen? Yes, this is the third time dealing not only with noncompliance of church mandated doctrines, but insubordination of superiors and the misuse of so-called supernatural gifts."

Dr. Davis, sitting at the head of the table spoke, "Brother Bill, we are not against the furtherance of the gifts that God has ordained, but..."

Third Board Member stood to his feet, "Pastor Davis, we cannot allow any further display of these...these visions, ghost dreams, fantasies...to continue. Especially, as a young and short timed member...as Branham is...to the ministerial board. It will leak out, sure as the world, and have fanaticism among the laity."

Dr. Davis took a deep breath and proceeded, "I shall lay it on the table. These sightings or trances are just a version of fortune-telling. It is merely the allowance of letting the mind to run wild. Psychosomatic behavior."

William was trembling, and with lips white with shock, he boldly spoke again, "Yes indeed, the occult needs to be with-stood, but for taking sides against direct scriptural commands concerning women preachers, and the visitations of God's angel... I'll save you the effort of your reprimand and seeking for recantations."

Reverend Branham reached into his pocketbook and threw his association card on the table and walked out.

CHAPTER SIX
A YOUNG PROPHET HAS COME TO THE U.S.

JEFFERSONVILLE
OLD BRANHAM HOMESTEAD

William rolled over in bed and was nervously tossing. He got up and started pacing the floor in the room. He turned toward a stuffed chair, and his vision split, and he saw himself outside walking.

VISION BEGINS.

William was way off stumbling about in a forest thickly wooded, listening, searching.

William said, "Now, just a moment. I'm not sleeping..., but it's so plain. I remember I was praying near the bed and... it came to me. This must be one of them..."

Down through the woods he stumbled on through the briars, thorns tearing at him. In the distant fog a little lamb could be heard bleating, "Baa, baa."

William, "Poor little thing, lost and alone in this darkness."

An Angelic voice spoke faintly, "Milltown...Milltown... then loader "Milltown"

VISION ENDS.

~

William staggered trying to clear his head. He half crawled and half fell back into bed.

JEFFERSONVILLE – BRANHAM CHURCH DAY

Reverend Branham is at the pulpit, dressed in a suit and tie, he asked, "Does anyone know where Milltown is?"

A man in the rear of the church raised his hand. Mr. Wright spoke up, "Yes, I live near there. It is south of here, near the Kentucky border."

MILLTOWN, INDIANA – ROAD TRIP DAY

Mr. Wright and Reverend Branham were traveling down the road when they came upon the sign for Milltown. The car slowed down near a little church, and they stepped out of the car. William looked the place over and said, "That's a nice old church overlooking the city, up high like this."

Mr. Wright, "It's the old Missionary Baptist Church building."

William, "What happened, it appears unoccupied?"

Mr. Wright said, "It's a story. Something went wrong few years back. A minister and folks got into a shooting scrap. The people just turned it over to the city for funerals and such, now." "I have to go up the hill to deliver some eggs...be right back."

William rambled over to the main door and tried the knob. Locked.

William bowed his head, "Lord, I don't know what to make of this. Please, direct my steps and open this door, if this is you."

He stepped away from the door and looked out upon the countryside and then faced the town. Someone came around the corner of the church, whistling a tune. A stranger made a few steps more and halted as he realized someone was standing there.

"Howdy, Preacher."

Reverend Branham, "Yes, oh…how did you know I was a preacher?"

MILLTOWN – BAPTIST CHURCH SUNDAY

Only the Stranger, Mr. Wright and his family showed up for morning services. William was leading in the worship song, "Blessed Be the Tie That Binds." A shabby man walked in late, looked around and carefully blurts out, "You that, Billy Sunday?"

Those at church are walking out and past where the Shabby man was standing. He waited until William exited the building. "I usually ain't got time for preachers, most of em' are hypocrites." William waited to hear what he had to say, "There is a young girl in these parts who hasn't been off her bed in nine years. Think you could go and… pray for her? She's been crying really hard, asking for you. Her folks go to that big church here and don't believe in such stuff. Don't know if they'll even have you. Carter is her name, Georgie Carter."

William has a flash back and heard the bleating again in the woods. He spoke in his mind, "There's that little sheep."

MILLTOWN – MISTER WRIGHT'S HOUSE – 1947

Mrs. Wright is busy preparing dinner and spoke up when William walked past the kitchen area, "It's just too bad about that little lady up there, never move off the bed. Brings me to tears." She uses her apron to wipe her eyes.

William spoke, "God will move. You just set still and let God do it. He'll work it out. I am going out to pray a spell."

Mrs. Wright, "Dinner be on, soon. We can ring the bell when it's ready."

William walked out into the evening setting sun. The woods were refreshing and he sighed and breathed in deeply. At a blown-down tree he knelt. Time is of no concern to him and quickly passes. A faint bell chimes and then another, two hours roll by. Shouts are faintly heard coming into the woods.

William prayed, "Oh God, have I done something wrong or is there anything I must do?"

A greenish light shined down through the Dogwoods and an Angelic voice spoke, "Go by way of the Carters." William got up and rushed back through the woods into Mr. Wright's arms, out of breath.

Mr. Wright, "Where have you been all this time? Mother's been keeping the food hot for hours."

William responded, "No time to eat now, it's, 'Thus saith the Lord.'" She'll be made every whit whole, in just a few minutes."

Mr. Wright's face was full of bewilderment. "You mean... that, that's from God?

GEORGIE CARTER'S PLACE

Mrs. Carter's face was full of tears, she grabbed her apron and wiped her face. She was kneeling on the kitchen floor.

Mrs. Carter prayed, "God, that reprobate Branham is going through the countryside here, got my girl all worked up. Poor thing, laying there dying. Oh God, put a curse on him."

While in prayer, she saw Jesus coming through the wall and it turned into the face of William Branham with a receding hair line, holding a bible. She got up and quickly ran to Georgie's room.

Mrs. Carter, "Honey, you know what…"

The screen door opened and shut very loudly. William entered the house. Mrs. Carter turned and met Reverend Branham in the living room.

Mrs. Carter, "I am so sorry… how I made such a fuss with you concerning my daughter. You just don't know what it's been like. Every so-called-healer and… just…"

Reverend Branham, "That's all right, Ma'am. Just, let's go in and… just a minute, shall we?"

Walking down the hall they entered the girl's room. Mrs. Carter knelt at the bed. Georgie, seventeen years old, was lying in bed, all thirty-eight pounds of her. Her eyes and skin were yellow. She was nothing but skin and bones. William leaned over to hear her speak.

Georgie spoke, "I heard a story about a girl named Nail, who had gotten heal'd. I heard how God had showed you that she would be healed…how her legs straightened out. I just know that God will show you something for me. I…I just do."

William, "Georgie, as God gave a vision of a little lamb trapped in the woods, crying out in desperation. He just met me down there praying. He told me to lay my hands on you and set you free."

He took hold of her hand, "In Jesus' name, rise up and be whole."

She rose to the bedside, then with a deep breath she started walking through the house, screaming. Her Mother threw her hands up to her heart and fainted away.

Georgie called out, "Oh, I must go outside."

Georgie went out the screen door and sat down in the grass and ran her hands through it.

Georgie lifted her face to the sky, "Oh God, how magnificent your name. Mighty are your works. Who cannot but sing and praise."

She got up and walked into the house, sat down at the piano and played, "Jesus, Keep Me Near the Cross." Some nearby neighbors heard the commotion and came over to see the miracle. Her Father came into the house with two other ministers and just stared on, as she played.

JEFFERSONVILLE, INDIANA
BRANHAM TABERNACLE
(Notes from 1955 The Approach to God)

Reverend Branham was speaking to the church of a vision he had, "A great White Steed prancing, remember, that's the WORD made flesh. Then shortly afterwards, up comes behind him or after him, comes this other fellow. He will be on a three colored horse, and not nearly as big as the first. On its neck reads, "Religious," on its stomach reads, "Political" and on his back haunches reads, "Demonic." The rider kept trying to bump his head...bump the White Stallion (rather) off of the trail. More on that, later."

William paused and cleared his voice, "Billy loves horses, too. I could speak for hours how he has shunned the voice of God, warning him. He has never made a full consecration; you know how kids are." "I was just thinking that not long ago, a well-known Minister said to me, "I would like to straighten you out on the Godhead." And I said, "I got time right now..."

Minister says, "You teach that there is just one God, I believe that there is, yes, one God, but in three Persons."

William says, "Would you repeat that again? Where did you go to school at? You cannot be a person without being a personality. If you are a personality, you are that solely to yourself."

Minister, "The theologians can't explain that."

William, "I should think not, but it's by revelation."

Minister, "I can't accept revelation."

William responded with, "How can God ever get to you? It's hid from the eyes of the wise and the prudent and unless Him revealing it, the result is a cold theologian. Melchizedek, had no father, nor mother, no beginning of days nor ending of life."

CHAPTER SEVEN
THE OBEDIENT PROPHET

JEFFERSONVILLE – BRANHAM'S HOUSE

William was out fishing along a creek with a fly rod. Five other men were scattered down the bank line, several meters away. The Angel of God spoke to him and His presence comes near. William had a few days of stubble sticking straight out. "As the Prophet of ol', was told to marry a prostitute as a type for this day, so too, marry Meda. I have a lesson to be revealed, in it."

Meda, now twenty-six years old was caring for the children. There were two little girls, and Billy Paul (twelve years old). Meda was combing Billy Paul's hair.

"You are sure growing up fast Billy, your shoulders are broadening out. Bet you will be a bigger man then your step...Dad..., your Daddy. Hope, your Mom... would've been proud of you."

Billy Paul turned and looked up to her with a smile. There is a moment of magnetism.

William Branham enters the house carrying a rolled-up paper. Meda quickly put the comb down and William called out to her, "Meda dear, would you put some clothes together for the meetings in Arkansas. I'll be heading out there right away. One of the managers sent me this newspaper. William opened the paper so she could read it. It read Arkansas Sun News. There was a picture of a lady lying dead, with sheet over her.

Meda Branham read out loud, "Died from colon, liver and heart cancer." Her last words were, "Just take me to the meetings of William Branham, whether I make it or not."

ARKANSAS – CHURCH PRAYER MEETINGS

The hallway was full as William made his way into the back of the church. A deacon came over with an urgent message. The deacon leaned over close and spoke with Reverend Branham, "There is a dead woman in the back office. They have been waiting for you...we didn't know what to do with her."

They entered the room to find a tall gentleman with his head hanging low.

William Branham, "Do you believe God can do this? To raise her up, whole again?" Gentleman, "Yes sir, we were in the prayer line a couple days ago but didn't get through. She told us to get her back in that line, to come before you whether she died or not. She died just..."

The gentleman started to cry.

William Branham, "Her faith was great. Let's pray a minute. 'Our gracious Father'..."

The lady lying dead on the cot, came to life. She reached up and pulled the sheet off from her face and raised up to a sitting position. Her husband rushed over to her and fell to his knees, looking up.

JEFFERSONVILLE – BRANHAMS HOUSE – 1947

Meda Branham was putting dinner in the oven. William was sitting reading a newspaper and turned to the religious section. His eyes scanned over a portion. Several comments were made from the Baptist Association regarding fanaticism creeping into their courts.

William, "Meda dear, I just don't know what I'm going to do. Listen to these statements from different ministers. Here's one from Dr. Davis. 'The sightings and or the proclamation of the supernatural phenomena in religious meetings are strictly spiritualism and anti-Christ. These ministers who have popped up recently, and who professes such abilities as to speak for God, seeing halos and Angels in the meetings, and knowing futuristic events, were strictly for the Apostles. It was the Apostolic Dispensation.'"

William got up rather disgusted and paced the floor, "Honey, I am rebuked, scoffed at, be-riddled, and challenged constantly about these visions I've been having. You know I don't go out seeking these things. I'm even afraid of getting a sharp reprimand for mentioning the Angel of God. You got enough here for you and kiddies, to hold you for a while. I am going out to the woods to find an answer, once and for all."

Meda stopped folding clothes and turned abruptly to him. "And you'll be back, when?"

She looked into his face seeking consolation. William stepped up to her and grabbed her arms.

William, "I...I'm not sure. Maybe I won't return, unless God speaks to me concerning these things. I'm going to Green's mill. Don't send for me."

GREENS MILL WILDERNESS – PRAYER CAVE

A backpack was stripped from William's shoulders and quickly set down on a log near a cave-type opening. He took down his rifle from the other arm and rested it against a log. He hasn't shaved in a couple of days and was wearing rough hunting garb. In his frustration and concern, he ran his fingers through his receding hair and dropped his hat beside him. A couple of squirrels came out of a hole in an old oak tree and played at the base of it. A mountain lion can be heard some distance away. William was heard praying.

William Branham prayed, "Oh Lord, you never forsook me, you are always near. You are all about me and your forests calm my anxiety…my questions..."

William was looking out over the valley from the bluff deep in meditation.

FLASH BACK BEGINS.

Meda Branham, "You're always going off and leaving me behind. You have never been home for any of our anniversaries. You don't love me like...like a husband ought, I need physical affection and my body...as any other woman. I am not made of stone. You're as celibate as a Monk. I need a man...not some god."

William, "I'm sorry that you feel that way. I do love you and cherish your companionship. I must be true to the commission and heavenly vision given to me."

FLASH BACK ENDS.

GREENS MILL – WILDERNESS CAVE NIGHT
(Seven days later)

William's beard had grown out. He was seen in the gathering darkness, sitting on a rock ledge with his head leaning against the rock wall. His eyes open, shut, then open again, as a light begins to radiate softly from near the cave opening. He sat up to hear if anyone was coming. The light brightened as it came forward. He was startled as a man's form stepped out of the brightness. William stared in shock, breathing hard.

Angel of God speaks, "Fear not, I have come from the presence of God to tell you of your strange and difficult life. You are to go to all the world and bring a gift of divine healing. You shall be brought before Kings, Monarchs and to the lost tribes of El Shaddai."

Prophet Branham, "I…I have been told that these visions and trances are…are of my own devices. That it is merely psychology and of the devil…witchcraft."

Angel of the Lord, "Remember how they rebuked, chided and blasphemed the Master planter? Did not the devils know who Jesus was? Remember him from Gadara that was bound with chains, and also, she who had a familiar spirit, which knew Paul. You are to be the evening sacrificial Ram, that was slain."

William fell to his knees.

Prophet Branham, "I won't be able to do this job for I am uneducated. I am a very poor man…pathetic really. No one will listen to me, why should they? Even the church board accuses me."

William, in tears, stood back up and paced. Nearby, the Angel is patient.

William, "I love the people of all races and of every nation, but they don't seem to be able to love me...my blunt speech. They resent what I try to share. My Mother is half Indian, but to them, I am a... white buffalo for sure, just odd to them."

Angel of the Lord, "As Moses was given two signs so shall you be given two signs. You shall take the people by the hand and vibrations and colors will come across your own, to show what diseases they have. If you remain sincere it will come to pass that no man's secrets shall be hidden from you. With visions I shall make my will known to you. I am the Almighty. Shall anything resist my will?"

William sweating, and again, fell to his knees in fear.

William Branham, "No Lord, nothing."

Angel of the Lord, "Nothing shall be impossible to you, not even cancer will withstand your prayer. You are my Prophet, my mouthpiece and final voice to all the world. Blessed is he who hearkens to the final voice, to the final age. Judgment is forth coming. I have chosen you to be Chief of the Remnant of the "Woman's Seed" and shall reign in Majesty with a rod of iron. You shall pray for kings and Potentates.

GREENS MILL WILDERNESS – TWO DAYS LATER

William came out from the cave and stirred the fire coals to life. He sat the coffee pot on the coals and stretched to his full height. He walked to the edge of camp and spoke out loud to himself, "As I review the wisdom of the ages, there is a wilderness of the soul and of the mind of man. Heroes have risen to the occasion time and time again, to ring liberty's bell and to raise freedom's banner for a short moment. Only to succumb to being ruled by yet another even more aggressive oppressor."

He moved back to the fire and stooped down to pour himself a cup of Java.

Reverend Branham, "Why this continual circle of rage for survival, for peace? Even the Holy Scriptures say, 'And there was war in Heaven.'"

The Angel of God appeared near the edge of the lookout bluff and spoke to him, "There is much for you to know."

William was startled and dropped the coffee pot while attempting to set it down. He turned toward the Angelic voice.

Angel of God, "Come with me and I'll show you the foundations of history. Come and see."

The Angel beckoned to William.

TIME TRAVEL VISION BEGINS.

EARTH'S HISTORY – KINGDOMS BEFORE TIME

The Angel of God and William were swept up into a vision and were floating above the scene taking place. William was sucked back into time, past the Crucifixion of the Christ, to the time of the prophet Isaiah.

Angel of God, "Unto us a child is given, a Son is born, and the government shall be upon His shoulders. His kingdom shall be without end."

The vision took him back past the parting of the Red Sea, the flood of Noah's time, the garden where Eve and Adam are seen unafraid and happy, eating of various fruits. The creation of mammals, reptiles, and fish. The land broke up into continents. The vision zoomed out away from the earth – traveling as the speed of light through, and away from the galaxies, and even they disappear. All Light goes out. Blackness. Silence.

God spoke, "Let there be light, the light of truth. That light that is the light of a Theophany-Christ Man."

An amber color began to glow. Amid a collage of collective and random shades of thought, light began to be born. From the far reaches of these thoughts moved the light of truth. From the infinitesimal to the great and holiest, gathered this light. Out and away from the face of deep pitch, came trickles of these thoughts down tributaries, then became streams, and streams into rivers. The river of the brightest light pools into an image of an Angel man, so intense as to not be steadfastly looked upon.

God spoke, "Out from pure light steps a Logos body, the first angelic Theophany-man. He is MELCHIZEDEK, one who had no father, no mother, no beginning or no end of life. This is Theophany Adam of Genesis, not he which is of the earth of chapter two but of chapter one. The Theophany Adam's face is the image of William Branham. **A SEAL SLIPS AWAY.**

~

A scroll sealed with Seven Mysterious Seals appeared – as the one found in the book of Revelation of the Christian bible – and came into view for all to see. With the untying or the unruffling of the first seal, a hidden mystery of the Melchizedek unwrapped itself and fell away.

TIME TRAVEL CONTINUES.

All around Him gathered shadow bodies of varying shades of color. The further away from Theophany Adam the different shades of the multitude of color, then darker shades of brown and then out into black, again.

THEOPHANY-ADAM, "Let there be lights in the firmament to divide darkness of evil from the brightness of truth. Let there be stars also to divide day from night."

The Light in the Universe began to intensify. Screams from the exposed darker spirit bodies were tormented by the Theophany Adam.

Lucifer (gray tint in color) speaks out, "All you who are willing to be tolerant of others' views, willing to compromise, regardless how shaded the lifestyle, come and fortify with me. All you stout fellows come bind together, lest we be cast out of our home."

An army of druid, dragons, Monarchs and Princesses with intoxicating allurements, all came and gathered at Lucifer's feet.

Lucifer continued, "We have tried to build our domain in the far reaches of heaven's shore, but alas, the glow of truth is ever disturbing our solace."

Over the ruckus, Theophany-Adam spoke out, "All are welcome to come and receive of me the light that will bring that creative power, life eternal. All other forms of life shall pass away. The Sons of God resist the evil and darkness. All evil and those who embrace the permissive will of God, shall eventually shrivel away into nothingness."

Theophany-Adam spread out his radiant arms and proclaimed, "Behold the creative power of God. Let there be stars and galaxies, also, let there be an earth, moons and planets."

The Earth and planets begin to appear. At first, one here and one there, then tens and hundreds appear at once.

Lucifer spoke, "Come, this obnoxious brilliance distracts my night life. Let us take up our festivities and fill the earth with love's songs of the night."

A roaring shout of exuberance and victory fills the air. From around the Throne of Heaven dark shadows and colored spirit bodies take their flight through space and hover over the Earth.

Lucifer urged them on, "See what a place as this can afford us all. All the pleasures and fancies our imaginations might conjure."

Simple Minded (pink in color) piped in, "It is sure to be a place of where every appetite may abound and be filled without restraint."

Covetous (green tint), "Let us grasp this domain, this instant. I shall have mine, and more."

Thousands of spirit bodies descended to the Earth. Theophany-Adam stood looking off to the Earth, which is flooded with water but then, as the waters receded, a lush garden with vegetation appeared.

Theophany-Adam, "Let there be...Let there be... Life begins to come forth upon the Earth."

As he beheld the creation he had made, he smiled. He is yet desirous of a creation much closer to himself. He looked within and saw, in his mind's eye, flesh man.

Theophany-Adam, "Let there be an ADAM-MAN made from earth's clay, and let him abide in the garden, east of Eden. Let him have a mind to make choices, a choice to love me, freely. That in time I may make him my image, my tabernacle."

Earth's soil began to heave up into the form of a man. Theophany-Adam blew with his mouth and a wind swept into Adam. Adam-man (20 years old) is tall and as hairy as the beast of the field. Adam-man was laid down again and from his side a woman was formed. Theophany-Adam spoke to EVE, "Thou shalt not partake of, nor touch the tree of knowledge, for it is the forbidden fruit that produces a life of continual death. The life from the woman's physical body is called perpetual life but is dead to eternal life."

Adam-man walked in the garden paradise and met up with Eve. Adam-man spoke, "I greet the fairest of all creatures. Your beauty ought to not go wasted without meeting the full potential of Godhood, that is, to your capacity in producing off-spring."

Eve, eager to hear more responded with, "Theophany-Adam tells me all I am to know, how is it that you – which are truly physically endowed can also tell of life's mysteries? Pray, do tell me more of which you speak."

Adam-man, "Have you not experienced that hidden power of sensuality that every beast of the field embraces? Are not every one of these producing from its own body, offspring? Allow me to bring stimulation and revealing. Allow me to touch you."

Adam-man and Eve are seen rolling on the grass in an embrace. Theophany-Adam, Eve's true husband approaches the scene. He said, "Who told you of your nakedness?"

Eve, "It is that slick talking serpent... (she pointed to Adam-Man) that Serpent Adam that beguiled me."

Theophany-Adam, "Because you have partaken of the two Trees fruit that brings life, you shall bring forth two different offspring."

Theophany-Adam turned to Eve, "The spoken creative seed that I give you, you shall call him, Able. Although he shall be a half-brother, he shall be at enmity with the Serpent Adam's seed. With Labor and sorrow shall you bring forth of that kind of seed."

VISION ENDS.

THE SCROLL APPEARED, RIBBON SEAL SLIPPED OFF AND FLOATED AWAY

The Angel and Reverend Branham returned to the Forest grounds.

ANGEL OF GOD, "Go back down from these mountains, the peoples need leadership."

CHAPTER EIGHT
MYSTERY OF THE REVELATION 10 MIGHTY ANGEL

JEFFERSONVILLE
THE BRANHAM TABERNACLE

Reverend Branham conversed with the Angel in the church office.

Angel of God, "Your ministry is that which Malachi the Prophet spoke, 'I shall send Elijah before the great and dreadful day of the Lord.' If you remain sincere, you shall fulfill Revelation chapter ten, Another Mighty Angel, also."

William, "Who am I to be the one to bring in a new Covenant for your people? I was going to leave the field because many have called me Jesus."

Angel of God, "I do a new thing. You shall indeed leave the field, as Prophet. As you have served well the office of son-of-man, so now, return in the office of Son-of-God. The whole Godhead is named Jesus.

The Angel summoned him to come, with a wave of His hand.

VISION BEGINS.

The Angel of God and William Branham are in Theophany bodies and are off to the side, watching the scene unfold.

Another Mighty Angel came down from Heaven which had the appearance of a man dressed in a white leather shirt and pants of a native American Indian Chief, but his face was four-sided. One side was that of a White Buffalo Calf, another was of a brown bear with a golden band around its neck, another is of William Branham, and the fourth of an eagle. A rainbow covered him. A whirling pillar-of-fire descended and caught all four images within the spin until William Branham stood alone.

Angel of God, "This exaltation shall surely come to pass. Be ever faithful and true."

William Branham, "Why is there a need for a second Covenant, since Jesus has already established one, 'Salvation of the soul,' by Grace?"

Angel of God, "As Moses smote the Rock the second time, so must the Son of Man be smote, once again. Jesus' Kingdom was not of this world but has returned to the Spirit dimension. However, the second son is to be transformed from the realm of the children of Serpent Adam, into that of the second coming of Christ. It is he, which is the true Son of David, not the first. He shall be the Royal Seed of Abraham."

William Branham, "Is that why you forbid that I go to Israel?"

Angel of God, "Israel is the title given to him that has wrestled with God and has over-came, as JACOB did in type. He is the Chief, the Corner Stone. As Revelation Chapter three states, 'I shall write upon Him my NEW NAME.' And again, in Chapter Nineteen, 'And I saw the heavens open, and behold a white horse; and he that sat upon him was called FAITHFUL and TRUE. And on his head were many crowns; he had a name written that no man knew, but himself.'"

To William Branham's amazement a white charger stepped out into view, with a prance. And he who rode him was dressed as a Native American Indian Chief, with a full Eagle feather headdress, a breastplate of bone and a great sword in his hand. On the horse's side was a banner written, The "WORD OF GOD." The rider took his horse through a pool of blood and came out the other side, stained red. The bloody rider is he who was able to become the Evening Sacrifice, according to ancient writ. The rider was William Branham.

Angel of God, "And on his thigh shall be written, "KING of Kings and LORD of Lord."

VISION ENDS.

CHAPTER NINE
ACTS OF A PROPHET

PORTLAND OREGON
MUNICIPAL AUDITORIUM – 1947

William Branham was standing at the pulpit, addressing the audience of six thousand, talking on the subject of faith.

William Branham, "Faith is not a 'hope so,' but a 'know so'…wait…a minute…ah."

William's vision began to blur. He stared off into space.

VISION BEGINS.

1. A seven-foot-tall angry man was lifting a preacher up over his head and throwing him out into the audience.

2. The same man was wrestling with police officers as they put him into a straight jacket at the sanitarium.

3. The insane man busts open the front doors of the Insane Asylum and made his escape.

4. The same man again, came up to a pulpit and with mighty blows, broke the collar bone and jaw of another minister.

VISION ENDS.

~

Reverend Branham shook his head slightly and blinked his eyes.

Reverend Branham, "Umm…I… something is going to…"

The large, enraged man which recently escaped the sanitarium rose up from the back row and moved swiftly to the platform. He began to curse and threaten William as he climbed the stairs. Three policemen moved forward to intercept the attacker. William Branham turned towards the police with his hand raised.

Reverend Branham, "No, please. He has challenged the Holy Ghost."

The officers reluctantly step back. Reverend Branham stepped away from the microphone and the insane man now towers over William. Spit is slung from the man's mouth as he raved towards William.

Insane Man, "I shall bust you up and throw you out into the crowd as I have done many times before. You messily little hypocrite. I'll show just how much of a man of God you are. You SERPENT."

William remained calm.

William Branham, "Because you have challenged the Spirit of God, you shall fall at my feet."

Insane Man, "I shall show you, who will fall, at who's feet."

The big man raised his fist to strike. His eyes seem to roll back into his head and his mouth opened wide. He bellowed. He then began to turn in circles and fell across Rev. Branham's feet. The policemen came up to take him away.

Police Man #1, "Is he dead?"

Police Man #2, "Is he delivered?"

Reverend Branham, "No, he's not dead and he is not delivered. He worships that spirit."

Stepping back to the pulpit he turned towards the crowd.

William Branham, "Our Heavenly Father has all power of Heaven and earth. All things are possible now."

A sick man lying on a cot cried out and raised up.

Man in cot, "Yes, he has. He has healed me."

Another man with crutches threw his crutches across the floor, shouting.

Man on crutches, "He has healed me, too!"

He began to walk and leap, unaided. A man stood up out of a wheelchair and hollered, "Me, also."

JONESBORO, ARKANSAS DAY
(Six months later)

Traveling from the St. Louis campaign, the William Branham car arrived on the church grounds of Bible Hour Tabernacle. The Police were sweating it out as they tried to direct traffic that has quadrupled in mass in just a few days. Several ambulances were already there.

Billy Paul (seventeen years old) craned his neck and got up on his tiptoes to see out into the crowd gathering. He spoke to couple of other young ushers in neckties.

Billy Paul, "Ya, but he isn't here just yet...somewhere out in the parking lot. Those who are willing to pay, give em' the numbers between twenty-five and fifty."

Usher Friend, "How much?"

Billy Paul smiles. "Those with serious cases, are willing to dish it out. We'll pool-it all, after the meeting."

William is just another of thousands as he walked among the crowd. Tents and canvas shelters were being erected all over town, against the rain. Pressing through the crowd, William heard a desperate cry of a young black lady, named Katrina. He entered the church parking lot looking for her.

Katrina (seventeen years old), "Daddy, Daddy."

The blind girl was bumping and pushing her way through the crowd. William was directed to the pathetic sight, for no one was paying her any attention. He stepped into her path, and she bumped up against him.

Katrina, "Excuse sir, please. I am blind and have lost my father, can't find my way back to da bus."

William Branham, "Where are you from? What are you doing here?"

Katrina, "I'm from Memphis, I come tu see da healah. I hear'd of him on the radio this morning. I hear'd of other folks born deaf and blind. Doctuh say dat the nerve is wrapped aroun' my eye. Dey say, dis here is da last night of meetings. My only hope is to see da healah."

Many people were taking notice of this. Why was a white man paying so much attention to this young girl. William's head was bowed, and he then lifted his face with tears running down.

Reverend Branham, "Do you believe these things you have heard, especially since all the fine doctors there are?"

Katrina, "Yes suh, da' doctuh's have failed to do anything and I believes the Angel that visited Parson Branham."

Reverend Branham, "Little lady, perhaps I am the one you are looking for."

She grabs him by the lapels.

Katrina, "Is you the healah? Please do not pass me by, suh. Have mercy on me, a blind girl."

William, "I am William Branham, Jesus is your healer. Let's pray. 'Lord, some 1900 years ago His frail body fell beneath the load of the cross he was carrying, when Simon of Cyrene, helped him carry it. Now, here is one of Simon's children standing here, staggering in the darkness. I'm sure you understand'..."

At that moment the girl screamed out. "I's can see. I's was blind but now I's see. I's see. I's can see."

The church ushers were trying to push through the crowd to get to William. The crowd then recognized William and rushed towards him. A man on crutches with a deformed leg hollered out, as William watched on.

Crippled man, "Brother Branham, I know you. I have been standing in the rain for eight hours now. Have mercy on me."

William, "Do you believe and accept me as God's servant?"

Crippled man, "I do."

William, "Then in the name of Jesus Christ, the Son of God, you're healed. You may throw away your crutches."

Immediately the crooked limb was made straight. He leaped and shouted. The crowd gathered around to touch him. The Ushers escorted William to the church. As he started to enter the building an ambulance driver pressed through and shouted.

Ambulance driver, "Sir, Sir, there is a woman in dire need of you, I believe she just died."

The driver was motioning for him to come over.

Two ushers were now surrounding Reverend Branham from the press of people trying to get to him.

One usher spoke out, "There are two thousand people who are in need, between him and the Ambulance. He cannot come to you just now."

William instructed the ushers to take him over to the ambulance now, and to the man.

Ambulance driver, "Sir, my patient has just died. Won't you come to her?" Entering the back of the ambulance William saw a man on his knees, in patched bibbed overalls.

Husband of the dead woman, "Brother Branham, Mother's gone."

Reverend Branham moved to take her hand.

William Branham, "She had cancer."

Husband of the dead woman was now crying openly, "That's true. Oh God, give me back Mother."

William was heard praying, "Almighty God... I beseech you in Jesus Christ's name to restore to this woman, her life again."

Her hand was seen gripping William's tightly, and he raised her up to sit. The husband gasps and grabbed hold of her.

Husband of dead woman, "Thank God. Mother, you're with me again."

The Ambulance is now surrounded.

JONESBORO, ARKANSAS
BIBLE HOUR TABERNACLE

William was in the pulpit speaking to a large crowd, "But now, he wants you to have a part in this, too. It is your faith pulling, that calls God into action...on the scene. Many claim to have faith, but all they got is a, hope-so. The Angel said, if I can get the people to believe on me, see?"

Pastor Richard Reed and two other ministers started a fast prayer line with William Branham. Several hundred were prayed for. A mother approached with a little girl of six or seven, and she was prayed over. She was wearing a body brace down her legs. She was a pretty child with one tooth missing in front. After a few minutes, William saw her coming through the line a second time.

William Branham, "Now, here honey, you just sit right over here and carefully watch for a while. You just sit there and pray.

The mother stepped off to the side of William with her daughter. He turned back to the line of people again.

William Branham, "He has to know his master, the Chief Builder. Bring them through now. 'As you believe on Christ, so receive.' 'God heal'd you of that stomach problem. Go eat your dinner.' In Jesus's Name be healed of that diabetes...."

William Branham's brother Donnie watched all this transpire from several feet away. He turned to a friend and whispered amongst the clamoring Prayer line and people rejoicing, "Ya, go figure. He put that real crippled little girl off to the side so he could just forget about her."

Reverend Branham turned toward Donnie.

Reverend Branham, "No Donnie, I haven't forgotten her."

The little girl was called over to stand behind William. She held to his coattail. He turned back to the prayer line and people started to rejoice when they could feel healing come over them. William then turned to the little girl.

William, "You're almost there, honey. Keep praying."

A few more minutes passed, and William turned around, "Now, Sweetheart, 'Lord, you see this little one's faith raise up high now. We praise you for healing her.'"

William turned to the mother. "Now, take the braces off her legs."

Mother of child, "But, Brother Branham, I tell you, she..."

William Branham, "Don't doubt that Lady, you just do what was said to do." He turned back to the others in the prayer line. In a minute the little girl walked over and presented the braces.

William Branham turned to Doctor Bosworth, "Doctor Bosworth, do you see this?"

William pointed to the little girl standing perfectly whole.

Doctor Bosworth, "I do. It is a miracle."

The Prayer line is still passing by. William looked over the audience and saw a vision of a young cowboy working with horses and was thrown off hard to the ground and had crippled his arm, for the last few years. He scans the balcony.

William, "Sir, you way back in the fourth row, going from this way, with the white shirt on. Stand to your feet. Jesus Christ has healed you."

The cowboy's wife started jumping up and down, screaming as his arm straightened out.

JONESBORO, ARKANSAS
BIBLE HOUR TABERNACLE HALLWAY

Doctor Bosworth escorted William Branham down the hallway, past many people.

Doctor Bosworth, "But how did you know it was that man?"

William Branham, "I felt myself getting weak from someone's pulling faith, and then I saw him fall from the horses back."

Doctor Bosworth, "Brother Branham, several men have come in just now and brought an insane patient, we put her down in the basement. Please, I believe it of interest, if you got a couple minutes. There has never been a case of its equal." The ministers directed Reverend Branham down the stairway to the basement. William was in awe of what he was saw when he stepped through the doorway. He was holding his bible under his arm. A man wearing over-bibs stood on the steps that led down to the lower level, the loading dock. A woman was laying on her back with her legs sticking straight up in the air. Her husband was fidgeting with his cap.

Reverend Branham stepped over to the farmer man, "How do you do?"

Farmer with bibs, "You, William Branham? She's a good woman, kind. She has been working hard out in the field with me, working to make a home and viddles...for the children."

William turned, "I understand. I'll go down and see if there are any vibrations."

Farmer with bibs, "Ain't safe. Don't go out there, cause she'll kill you."

He came to the bottom of the steps and walked out to her and looked down into her face. Her eye lids were batting fast. He spoke soft words and reached down to her and carefully took her hand. Her hair was matted and was covered with months of soiled filth. Her dress was in rags.

Farmer with bibs, "She doesn't even know her name, hasn't for years."

Without any signs of warning, she had caught hold of William and jerked him so hard it lifted him off balance. He stumbled forward. She then pulled him way down to her, but he reacted in time and placed his foot against her chest. He gave a quick yank and pulled free to step back to the stairway. She chased him like a snake on her back. She then grabbed hold and pulled a steel bench loose that was bolted to the wall, and threw it, barely missing her husband. Chucks of concrete flying. The woman's legs were badly cut up.

William Branham, "Why are her legs so bloody?"

Farmer with bibs, "We had six men to put her in the

ambulance, but we couldn't hold her. She kicked the windows out of the station-wagon, coming down here. The glass..."

Fresh blood ran now where the bench must have hit her head while she was throwing it.

Insane Woman, "E-e-e-e-e, e-e-e-e."

Reverend Branham, "God have mercy on a soul that is so bound, like that."

The big farmer started to cry. He walked over to William and draped an arm around him.

Farmer with bibs, "I just don't know what to do. I sold the farm to pay for expenses. The two mules I sold to get her here to the meetings. We got five children in need of their mother."

Reverend Branham, "God can heal her, for sure."

Insane Woman, "You have nothing to do with me. I brought her here."

Farmer with bibs, "Why, that is the first time she ever...?"

Reverend Branham responded, "The devil is just using her lips, as the case of Legion, in the bible."

William turned to her husband, "Brother, do you believe the story you heard me tell about the coming of the angel?"

Farmer with bibs, "With all my heart."

William turned to the woman and prayed out loud, "Oh God, have mercy on this little lady of five children. What can happen? Oh Lord, hear me as I pray. Satan, you are exposed now. Come out of her and let her go free, in Jesus's name."

William turned back to the farmer. Farmer with bibs, "I believe it with everything in me. What should I do?"

Reverend Branham, "Take her back. Take her right back to the sanitarium. If you don't doubt one thing that I told you, watch what happens."

ARKANSAS – ELDORADO MEETINGS
(Some months later)

Outside the church the ushers and two policemen escorted William out to the vehicles. People were pressing in from all sides. The ushers had a hard time maintaining forward progress. Amidst the clamor, a voice can be heard calling out for help.

Older Black Man, "Mercy, mercy, mercy." William heard a faint cry and paused. Again, he heard the call for help, "Mercy, mercy, mercy."

The older gentleman with just a white rim of hair around his head, along with his wife, were pleading. Rain was falling. The couple were standing outside the taped-off area of segregation. A piece of canvas was spread out over the William Branham's procession. Umbrellas and newspapers were held up to cover the women and children.

Reverend Branham, "I want to go over there, to that black gentleman, there."

William pointed out to the side of the crowd.

First Policeman, "You can't do that. You'll start a racial riot. There are still segregation laws that people hold to. You just can't do that."

Reverend Branham, "But the Lord is telling me to go over where he's at."

William saw their resistance to the idea and turned out of the processional. With the reluctant police escort trailing, he walked over to them.

Wife of the Blind Man, "Here comes the parson Honey. My, oh my."

Blind Man, "Are's you da man by name, Parson Branham?"

William replied, "Yes, sir."

Blind Man, "Parson, you just gots to hear'd dis, my story."

The ushers and policemen came over and spread the canvas back over the little group. The old gentleman raised his hands and felt William's face.

Blind Man, "Parson, my old Mammy was good religious woman. She never told a lie in her life. She had religion like your kind of religion. She's been dead and gone, going on ten years now. I's never did hear'd of you in all my life, even. Last night, I woke up and there by my bed stood my Mammy. She says, Honey child, you goes down to El Dorado, Arkansas and ask for someone by name of Branham. The Lord's gift of divine healing was given to him. You shall receive your sight."

William Branham, "Sir, the Lord Jesus that sent you that vision is standing here now to make you whole."

Blind Man, "I thank yu Lord, I's thank yu, Lord."

William turned to leave and their voices faded out.

Wife of Blind Man, "Does yu see, honey?"

Blind Man, "Yes'um, I sees."

A TRAIN BOUND FOR FLORIDA

William was standing at a window of the train car as it rolled down the track. The window disappeared as a vision scene began of two little boys who got ran down by a speeding car.

VISION BEGINS.

The Angel of God came to stand beside him. A vision appeared before him of a car accident where a little child was killed.

Angel of God, "Can the boy live?"

William saw himself kneel and place his hand on the child. The youth came back to life.

VISION ENDS.

~

The Angel then disappeared as he gained his focus and presence back inside the train, and he saw the countryside as it passed by.

JEFFERSONVILLE, INDIANA
BRANHAM TABERNACLE – 1948

William was at the pulpit speaking, "I would like to have you write down in the flyleaf of your bible, a vision I had while on the train; for those who have a pen. I saw two boys hit by a speeding automobile. One boy was hit and flew up against a tree and the other went under the car and was killed immediately. I saw the landscape was rugged mountains, lots of trees. The boy had brown hair and about eight years old. He wore suspender knickerbocker type shorts, with long stockings. Something you might see in Europe or Scotland or something. His shoe was off, and his little foot was sticking out of his sock. Terrible. But I have, 'Thus saith the Lord', the child will be raised back to life."

William was leaving the building when a woman came up all excited.

Insane Woman approaches, "Brother Branham, do you remember me?"

William, "No ma'am"

The Insane woman's husband laughs.

Farmer with bibs, "I took her back to the sanitarium and three days later they released her. She's completely healed."

Insane Woman, "I just want to give God praise for what He has done for me."

William Branham, "Go with God's blessings, for you and your children."

OUTSIDE KUOPIO, FINLAND – DAY – 1949-50

Three vehicles were rolling down the country road. William Branham, several ministers and Mrs. Issacson, were in route to another meeting. As they got near the city, the car they were following some-minutes ahead, swerved trying to avoid two boys playing while crossing the street. One boy dashed back in one direction while the other appeared to have made it across to the other side. The car hit both boys. A crowd quickly formed. The one boy is alive and is taken immediately to the hospital. The crowd moved in around the dead boy. People were weeping. The Branham party got out of the vehicles and joined the onlookers. Mrs. Issacson looked in on the site and returned to the car where Rev. Branham remained.

Mrs. Issacson, "Brother Branham, you, I'm sure, will want to see this. Please."

William got out and headed to the group huddled around a form with a cloth over his head. The cloth was removed and William's face turned pale. He began to turn away but stopped and looked again. His face changed as recollection came to him.

William Branham, "It's him. yes, I'm sure of it."

William turned to the members of his ministerial party. "Brothers look in the flyleaf of your bibles to see if this child matches the description of the prophecy. This is the child God will raise from the dead. See the rocks and the evergreen trees? Isn't this him?"

A couple of men head to the car and returned with their bibles. They returned and with a finger on the page.

Gordon Linsey, "Yes, it sure seems exactly the vision, even the sock tore off."

The crowd grew larger. William Branham stood to his feet and straightened up tall.

Prophet Branham, "Thus Saith the Lord. This boy shall raise up from the dead or I'm a false Prophet, and you can kick me out of your country."

The child stirred and was assisted to sit, then he began to stand. The crowd was in a state of unbelief, then began to gasp and tremble, some covered their mouths, and some dropped to their knees.

JEFFERSONVILLE
BRANHAM CHURCH OFFICE – 1949

Billy Paul (17 years old) grabbed the phone. Billy Paul Branham spoke, "Hello, is DOCTOR BEST in please? This is WCC headquarters? Yes, I'll wait."

Doctor Best came to the phone. Billy Paul, "Yes, this is Billy Paul Branham…, yes sir. It is even worse than before, no matter what others try to share with him. It's like my Dad is…"

Doctor Best, "It's like he has gone solo, refusing to cooperate. I am going to challenge him to an open debate. Just hold steady son, keep us posted on any changes. Ok, bye."

SAM HOUSTON COLISEUM – JANUARY – 1950

Reverend William Branham was at the pulpit testifying, "I had time to kind of get away…, fish, and go to my cabin in the hills to pray. The Angel told me I needed to be more sincere; that there would be a time where I would know the secrets of the heart, through discernment."

The congregation sat up in their seats.

William Branham, "Now, God is bringing in the second-pull type of ministry. The Angel himself will come and stand with me to discern the hearts, as they come. Now, I take every spirit under my control."

Beginning a prayer line, the patients came one at a time. A young man, Peary Green (sixteen years old) was on the front row watching every move. A man and a young child approached the Prophet.

Prophet Branham, "I see sir, that you come here on account of this child. He is obviously blind. Bring the little fellow here. Heavenly Father, I remember my little girl in so much pain that her little eyes crossed. Lord, you went to the cross so this child could go free. Satan, come out of the child."

The child faced his father and saw the tears streaming down, which the youngster then traced them with a finger on his father's face.

Peary Green had his mouth open and exhaled. The next person was a young woman holding a child with clubbed feet. Reverend Branham reached out and took the child.

William Branham, "Please remove the stockings."

The mother did as she was told. Peary Green can see that there was just stubs there. He leans closer to the platform.

William Branham, "Bow your heads as we pray."

Peary Green dips his head but looks carefully through his brows.

Reverend Branham, "Heavenly Father, I...."

Young Green's eyes bulge as Rev. Branham apparently

dropped the child to the floor, and he watched as two feet were created right before his eyes. The crowd gasped, cried out and shouted. The next patient was a young woman. Reverend Branham faced her, then quickly turned to the audience again.

Prophet Branham, "I have been careful to explain, that as you come to the platform, that you must repent of any sins. I cannot be responsible what is said under discernment." William Branham turned back to the lady. "Young lady, you have been unfaithful to your husband."

The audience became deathly still. A young man shouted out and began to run forward. The ushers stepped forward.

Prophet Branham, "That's her husband, let him come."

The young man stopped some twenty feet short of pulpit and was about to say something.

Prophet Branham, "And what about you and a red-headed secretary, last Friday night at the motel?" The young man froze.

William Branham continued, "You have not sinned against God but to your marriage vows. What you need to do is go around the curtain there and apologize to each other and renew your vows."

10

CHAPTER TEN
A HOUSE DIVIDED

SAM HOUSTON COLISEUM – JANUARY 22, 1950

Newspapers from all over the city were declaring of the Evangelist William Branham and teacher Dr. Bosworth's campaign. Brother Bosworth was teaching on Divine healing before the main service.

On the back row, a man (Rev. Best, of the Baptist Pastor's conference) stood up and stomped out.

HOUSTON NEWSPAPER PRINTERS
JANUARY 23RD

Newspapers were rolling out declaring, "Ecclesiastical fur will fly," a challenge by Rev. Best against Evangelist William Branham, with the focus of Divine Healing was meant for the Apostles only, but no longer. The post from Doctor Best also declared that "Branham," was a fraud and deceiver.

BAPTIST PASTOR'S CONFERENCE ROOM

Rev. Best is ranting about William Branham's Divine Healing campaign. Several others are in the room.

Doctor Best, "This impostor actually broadcasts his ability of Divine Healing. We need to put a stop to it, now.

Run him out of town, and I ought to be the man to do it. I have put a challenge in the paper yesterday, for William Branham to face me in a public debate."

SAM HOUSTON COLISEUM – JANUARY 24TH

Reverend Raymond T. Richey was the mediator, and each speaker would be given the same amount of time to make their case. The two contestants came out onto the stage. William Branham was in the balcony sitting quietly.

Doctor Bosworth, "I make a proclamation that the bible speaks emphatically of the promises pertaining to Divine healing, is the same today as it was yesterday. That Jesus' power is available to whom-so-ever-will and is core to the believer's heritage. How many in the audience tonight has had God touch you with the miraculous Redemptive power?"

Hundreds raised their hands.

Doctor Bosworth, "Good, then I want you all to come down here, and sit in these chairs reserved, up front. Yes, all who have been healed, come forward."

Hundreds began to move forward. Rev. Best became obviously agitated. Bosworth sat down.

Rev. Best began to preach, "Jesus breathed upon them, and they received the power of the Holy Ghost as the licks of fire anointed them. We have not had that commission nor out-pouring since that time, for it was exclusively for his Apostles only."

Doctor Bosworth jumped off his stool and ran to the microphone and rang out, "How many here have had God's blessings of Divine Healing? Stand to your feet." Hundreds stood, applause and ruckus stirred the audience.

Rev. Best turned red in the face and nearly yelled into the microphone, "The succession of a five-fold was handed down by those they appointed, and laid hands on them, giving them the power to preach and teach. Jesus never placed any such order where a man could act as if he had the authority to bring healing. Why don't you just bring that Divine healer here. No, you won't do that. Bring that divine healer here."

Doctor Bosworth, "It is not correct to place a label on Reverend Branham, of "Divine Healer," just as it would be for me to call you a "Divine Savior," just because one may believe in the soul's salvation."

Rev. Best, "Have him come out here and let's see him perform."

Doctor Bosworth, "That sounds a whole lot like, 'come down off the cross and we'll believe you.'"

Doctor Bosworth turned to the audience, "Let me see, by the upraising of your hands, how many knows that Jesus is the same today as yesterday, because of your Divine healing that you have had? "

The clock on the wall showed that three hours had passed. Rev. Best stepped over to Doctor Bosworth.

Rev. Best, "Here, come here you photographers. Let us take a couple pictures of this great man of God that performs these so-called mighty healings." He then pointed his finger under Doctor Bosworth's nose. "Ya, take this one too," as he placed his fist under Bosworth's chin.

A small scuffle started in the audience then quieted down as Rev. Richey came forward and spoke. "We have heard that Reverend Branham is in the audience, and I would like for our Brother to come at this time to close the service tonight."

Rev. Branham made his way to the platform and stepped up to the mic, "Good evening, friends. It certainly is a grand privilege to be here with you tonight. Wonderful cooperation and topic we are having, on whether God still does the supernatural in Divine healing or not. It is late for it to be questioned, because we have many, many years down the road of infallible proofs. Jesus is the same today as he ever was and ever shall be. What would we need Divine healing for when we're in the Millennium? We need it now, cause we won't be needing it then...when we are in glorified bodies."

The photographer snapped another photo of William Branham.

CHAPTER ELEVEN
THE TRAP IS SET

TEXAS
SOUTH WESTERN BIBLE COLLEGE
1950

Billy Paul Branham (seventeen years old) stepped through the door of the Dean's office. His mannerism and appearance were deceiving; maturity and eloquence have been his pursuits.

College Dean, "Furthermore, I know of many such ambitious, 'anointed ones,' but scripture makes clear we are to be wary of such ones and guarded. Gifts are often illusory; callings must be based upon the established institutions and delegated officials; else rampant usurpation is inevitable."

NEW YORK CITY
MEETINGS

William Branham took a trip to New York for a convention. He dressed in a three-piece pin-striped suit. He was addressing an audience which were in great anticipation of God working wonders through this small humble man. The congregation was packed-out and standing along the walls. Hands of many were raised and the faces were exuberant to respond. The music gave-way to the speaker.

William Branham, "We are to go now directly to Africa for a group of meetings. Our precious brothers there have always welcomed God's Holy Spirit, not like us starchy white Americans. Colleges – and the like – constantly oppose God's election and anointed God-sent men. Now, be in prayer for us because the Angel of God told me that there was a trap set. The Lord has definitely gone beyond our greatest expectations, standing against those who would bring ridicule and shame to us, by vindication of his power. Who all was at the Houston debate?" Many raised their hands.... "let us close in a word of prayer."

Reverend Branham was next seen walking into a New York city hotel lobby and picking up the phone to call the Bible College. "Hello Billy, I have several meetings arranged for overseas, right away, and would think it advantageous to have you join us. What do you say?"

Billy Paul can be heard responding back, "Rather sudden for immediate answer, can I call you back tonight?" Billy was seen entering the Dean's office.

College Dean, "Well, if you have already made the decision. Perhaps, you can help us, that is the Ministerial Association, by keeping us informed on his teachings, the way he sways the audience, his (behind the scenes) supernatural phenomena, et cetera."

Billy Paul, "That is certainly doable, will do."

College Dean, "Keep one thing in mind, redemption and all its benefits are not solitary given, but to everyone that believes. You have the same authority and power, as he." He turned to leave the office smiling.

JOHANNESBURG, SOUTH AFRICA
AIRPORT

Several ministers including Doctor Bosworth, William Branham and Billy Paul were coming through the door into the terminal. William Branham was greeted with a small party of men holding a banner of "Welcome William Branham." Brother Jackson and his wife also stepped forward to shake hands in greeting.

Billy Paul stepped away and was greeted by a gentleman with a highly polished appearance. They moved off to the side speaking confidentially.

Highly Polished, "We here at the ministerial association really didn't know how to respond and are a bit hesitant to get on board with the campaign."

Billy Paul shrugs, "Understandable. Daddy is no real threat…, I don't think. However, he is declaring that his doctrine is strictly God sent, with the suffix, 'Thus saith the Lord.' We both know his, 'thus saith the Lord' is a tool as vindication of his stand. After all, who can oppose God's word?" Billy Paul chuckled and Highly Polished guffed.

Highly Polished stepped away from Billy Paul and moved to a nearby phone stand. He made a hasty call fumbling the rotor dialer in his hurry. "Hey, this is Me. I have it from Billy Paul that William Branham is moving in different directions from the board. He's all about his own direction. He told me that he is now using the term, 'Thus saith the Lord' as a suffix to his doctrinal teachings."

A muffed response was heard.

Highly Polished, "Right."

Highly Polished hung up. Turned to leave but paused and turned back around. He then put another coin in the phone machine.

Highly Polished snapped out, "Be informed that William Branham and his party have arrived. They are to receive no cooperation. He is 'anti', on every ground."

JOHANNESBURG, SOUTH AFRICA
OUTSIDE CAFE

A young minister from the Dutch Reform church greeted a friend of his, who dressed quite distinguished and had a Billy Graham demeanor.

Young Minister, "He has just arrived from the U.S. for some divine healing meetings."

Distinguished Friend, "I've heard. Firstly, in order to be divine healing, it has to be ordered of God. I have heard of him through the Counsel – it, they tell it that this guy is like, way out there. Why, he's nothing but a polished-up soothsayer."

Young Minister, "I'm afraid that we will miss our day of visitation if we don't..."

The Distinguished Friend started to leave. He turned around to face his friend, while still walking away, and pointed a finger up, "Take it from me, a friend, that guy's a demon."

Young Minister called out to him, "I will go and pray for you...for that comment."

The distinguished friend turned around in-stride and took no more than a dozen steps when a burning sensation struck his shoulder. He flinched and looked over his shoulder and instinctively reached up to discover that his white shirt has a burned imprint of a hand on it. He rushed back to meet his friend again.

Young Minister, "Let's go, I know where he's staying."
They jumped into a cab. The city transit sedan arrived at

the hotel and the two men got out, ran up the few steps, and went in. As the door opened William Branham was there in the lobby to greet them.

Distinguished Friend, "I have been a critic of yours, but something has just happened to me that you might help with. "

He turned his shoulder to expose the print on his shirt.

Young Minister chimed in, "Brother Branham, would you check this out, what could it mean? It's a rather small handprint. Would you put your hand up here, just, just to..."

William Branham raised his hand to the shirt – it was a perfect match.

JOHANNESBURG, SOUTH AFRICA MEETINGS – 1951

William Branham came out on the platform before a large audience of about forty thousand.

Reverend Branham, "Greetings, to you friends from our Lord Jesus. I'm so happy for the success we have had here with you. Your faith has risen until just anything is possible. Billy is here somewhere; I told him the other day that he was..."

William Branham continued to look out across the audience. His eyes began to focus on two scenes at once, which then zoomed in onto a vehicle out of control.

VISION BEGINS.

A green car was spinning around with a young lady inside. Screams. Three men took her out of the car. The x-ray showed three broken places in her spinal column.

VISION ENDS.

Prophet Branham, "I..I..wait just a moment."

William Branham searched the audience of many thousands then continued,

"Pardon me, I just saw a young lady that was in some type of accident…car wreck of some kind. A drunk driver swerves. I see her spinning out of control, then running off the road and she strikes a tree." He continued to look out in the audience in search of her. He was drawn to look down. He stepped forward to the edge of the platform and then he saw her lying on a cot straight down off the platform.

Reverend Branham, "Lady, young Lady, you speak English?"

She nodded her head slightly.

"Wasn't it you in an accident…in a green car and hit a tree and it's broken your back?"

The young lady responded, "That's right."

Prophet Branham, "Thus saith the Lord, stand to your feet, you're healed"

The mother of the young lady jumped to her feet with a strong retort, "Oh, no, no. The doctor says if she moves it'll break her spinal cord and she'll die right here."

The young lady slowly raised up from the cot and declared, "Looky here."

The mother gasped and passed out in faint on the same cot the girl just got up from. Reverend Branham was back at the pulpit.

William Branham, "Now children, I would like...to"

His eyes began to blur over, and his vision splits again from the congregation onto a passenger bus with a large vinyl banner on it.

VISION BEGINS.

Reverend Branham's Theophany looked out. He saw a bus driving through the jungle with "Durban" written in bold letters on the side of it. As it stopped a boy got on board with a leg six inches shorter than the other. He was wearing a metal brace around his leg that supported the foot. Then he saw the boy walking normally without the support.

VISION ENDS.

~

He began to look out into the crowd. Through an interpreter, he spoke to the crowd. He then recognized a boy and pointed out towards his direction and asked, "Aren't you from Durban, Yes, you there on those crutches."

The young boy of about eight years old said, "Yes."

Reverend Branham, "You were born with one leg that is six inches shorter than the other?"

The young boy responded, "That's right."

William Branham stood erect, "Get up, Jesus Christ heals you, for 'Thus saith the Lord,' I've seen a vision, and you are healed."

The young lad quickly tore the braces off and stood to his feet normally and walked.

JOHANNESBURG, SOUTH AFRICA MEETINGS
HOTEL HALLWAY

Ern Baxter and Highly Polished spoke to Billy Paul outside their rooms.

Billy Paul tweaked his mouth up and raised his brow a bit, "The show must go on. If it is a schedule that was already agreed upon, then by every means proceed, certainly. He will have to go."

He flicked his cigarette away.

JOHANNESBURG, SOUTH AFRICA
HOTEL ROOM

It was the fourth morning of the meetings and William Branham was deep in prayer. The clock read a little after two o'clock in the morning. He was then startled by the Angel of God standing in the room.

Angel of God, "Do not go with those men. Stay here two weeks. Go hunting with Junior Jackson. This will let them know that they are not to go."

As the sun cut over the tree line the men of the Branham party are rousting and making their way downstairs with their luggage. There were twelve men in all to help promote and minister at the meetings.

Ern Baxter, "Good morning, Brother Branham, I trust you had a goodnight's sleep and you're ready for the road trip?" Reverend Branham was sitting in an easy chair, drinking coffee.

William Branham, "I am not sure what you are speaking of. Road trip?"

Ern Baxter, "The committee and our associates with us, agreed to move on now to Cape Town. Thousands are showing up for the promotions, tent, and settings.

Oh, that will be a real meeting with thousands to attend. Brother SCHOEMAN is a powerful man and can make things really click."

William Branham, "But we are having tremendous success here. God is pouring out his blessings out and we need to stay here."

Doctor Bosworth stepped up to them and injected, "As the manager of the Africa trip meetings, schedules must be kept, promises must be held."

William, "The Angel of God met me, and told me not to go, but to stay here another two weeks. I am to meet Brother Jackson and go hunting with him. I'm to stay here, then go up to Durban for a month. It's God's will that we stay here."

Others stepped into ear shot. Doctor Bosworth, "Perhaps God will let us move with His permissive will, if not his perfect will."

A round of chuckles resounded as Reverend Branham stared in shock.

Ern Baxter, "Say, David DuPlessis has it all set up, the whole itinerary."

Most of the ministers were now gathering outside the hotel waiting to take off on the trip. William Branham was still sitting down on an easy chair. Two more ministers overheard the commotion and moved over to them. Billy Paul (sixteen or seventeen years old) is standing near the two men, looking in.

Billy Paul, forcefully said, "Don't you realize that these other men are also used by God. They were appointed to make this itinerary; they are men directed by the Holy Spirit. The five-fold ministry is still in effect."

Reverend Branham, "I cannot say what God said to them, I just know what he spoke to me, last night. Not to go. I can't."

Ern Baxter took a sip of coffee and snidely replied, "Are you willing to take it to the Ministerial board?"

William Branham, "You mean that you'll ride right over what God said, not to do?"

SOUTH AFRICA
BUILDING FOR RELIGIOUS AFFAIRS

The door opened with a name plate, "National Committee," William Branham was escorted into the chambers with a large table facing several occupied stuffed chairs. The meeting got right into the heat of things without many formalities.

Committee's Chairman, Rev. Schoeman, "Yes, we do acknowledge the miraculous deeds done as true Divine healing. Undisputed. As a gesture of our deep appreciation, our cities have an open door to you, campaign managers and staff. However... in the best interest of National safety and security, we must maintain certain protocol."

All around the room there was the shaking of heads and smiles of approval. Reverend Branham looked around the room.

Committee's Chairman, "An up-rising of any kind can jeopardize our position and influence to the political powers. Showing favoritisms, and indiscreet appearances tend to fuel rioting...tribal restrictions. Therefore, you must conform with the scheduling David DuPlessis and associates have submitted. No argument will be admissible at this time."

William Branham left the room upset and mumbled, "How totally ridiculous, just while God is moving so powerfully. Just mess with preachers if you want trouble. They'll go through with their schemes, no matter what."

BRANHAM PARTY ROAD TRIP TO CAPETOWN

The drive took them through Kimberley where they wanted to stop and buy some keepsakes.

William spoke to a car full of ministers, "So you will know that we are out of God's will, firstly, a native will be standing with a long purple shirt gown. Then you will see a girl selling beads on the roadside. A patch of hair gone from the side of her head. After, Mr. Baxter will call our attention to large funny looking bird. By this you will know that you are not to take the itinerary the ministers have worked up."

The Branham party were casually walking the street mall. The girl with the patch of hair missing passed by, holding an armful of goods to sell. There was then a loud squawk and a large peacock flew overhead above the street market.

ROAD TRIP – HEADING FOR CAPETOWN

Brother Schoeman and his wife were in the front seat of the car with William Branham in the back. They were driving and William was nervous. He showed perspiration and was squirming some. The Angel of God spoke to Reverend Branham.

Angelic voice, "Are you going to listen to me?"

William almost jumped out of the seat.

William let out a little sound, "Ooh."

Mrs. Schoeman asked, "Are you ok, Brother Bill?"

William Branham, "Brother Schoeman, stop the car. Just stop. I can't go any further."

The car slowed to a stop. The other autos in the group do the same.

Brother Schoeman, "Brother, he is the chairman after all, he has the agenda and the ministers will not listen to that."

Reverend Branham, "That may be so, and they may have an agenda, but I'm going to listen to God, anyhow."

The Angel spoke to William, "Here's that trap, that was set."

Mr. Schoeman got out and walked back to the other vehicles. Doctor Bosworth, Brother Baxter and others met him.

Brother Schoeman, "He refuses to go farther." Ern Baxter walked up to the window of the first car.

Ern Baxter, "We are twelve thousand miles from home and at the mercy of these people. Don't you think you ought to consider the other ministers?"

The elderly Bosworth came over to the car. William Branham got out and stood forlornly.

Brother Bosworth said, "Now Brother Branham, I believe you're wrong on this."

William looked up into Doctor Bosworth's face, hurt like, a tear running from his eye.

NEAR A CAPETOWN, SOUTH AFRICA HOTEL

William Branham was in his pajamas sitting on the bedside, crying. He whispered, "Wow, what have I got into this time? What in the world am I to do? I got no money to stay here or to get another return flight ticket. The Lord was emphatic about me staying here. He is doing the miraculous here...No, I can't go with them, that's for sure. But Billy Paul and... we don't have..."

The Angel of God suddenly appeared. "You seem to be in quite a mess. This is that trap shown to you a while back, in the States. I give my permission for you to go with them, but you will pay for it dearly."

KIMBERLEY – HOTEL ROOM – NIGHT

The following day Ern Baxter, Billy Paul and Brother Bosworth came pushing through the door soaking wet and wind worn. William Branham stood from a lobby chair, as they entered.

Doctor Bosworth, "Worst night of the year, maybe since history began."

Ern Baxter, "We didn't hardly open the service and all hell broke loose. Pardon the French."

Doctor Bosworth cleared his throat and reported, "Tomorrow night will be different. We will have the abundantly and glorious, from the Lord. Many hundreds will see the mighty works of God."

The following night William Branham was in the lobby getting a cup of coffee when the hotel manager greeted him.

Hotel Manager, "Aah, Reverend Branham, I wanted to express my deepest appreciation for the pleasure of having your party in our humble hotel."

William Branham, "Good Evening."

Hotel Manager with all smiles said, "Strange change in the weather is it not? This violent cold wind sweeping through, cuts one to the core."

The clock read ten thirty in the evening. In walked the same threesome but this time obviously chilled to the bone. Ern Baxter was flapping his arms around his chest. "Oh, my word, Brother Bill, the service had to be closed due to a Northerner blowing in from the Artic, I swear."

William smiled, "What? It wasn't the abundant outpouring of God's blessings you all predicted? Now, now, gentlemen don't be too badly discouraged. After all, God did already tell us we would be out of his Will. But do come and have some hot coffee, it'll calm your nerves and lift your spirits."

KIMBERLEY – HOTEL LOBBY

Several guests and ministers were in the lobby getting coffee and preparing for the day. William Branham was walking down the stairs into the lobby; he looked weak and yellowish. He put his hand to his stomach. He was faint and staggered. Billy Paul rushed over.

Billy Paul, "Daddy, you alright?"

The other brothers caught his fall. Reverend Branham looked up into their faces.

"I told you; He said, He would make me pay for it. He will not be mocked. This is not the "abundantly." I need to go to Durban."

DURBAN – GREYVILLE RACECOURSE – 1951

William was escorted through a packed crowd towards the center of the racetrack stadium. He was lowered onto the platform by a rope to avoid the pushing masses. There are two hundred thousand people and growing. They were being led by a young man on all fours who had a collar around his neck and a chain was hooked up to him. He started to jump around and do doing antics. William spoke to an interpreter.

William Branham, "No, no, you have a brother you are thinking about right now, who is on crutches. He, as a child was riding a wild goat and was thrown off. He became crippled. God has healed him."

The young, chained man started rejoicing and hopping about. Through the crowd came a young lad holding his crutches in one hand, and who ran to the platform and embraced his brother. Reverend Branham turned towards the chained young man that was on all fours, "Stand to your feet, Jesus has healed you." The interpreter repeated it. William grabbed the man and helped him to his feet. Tears were running down his face and chest. Thousands fell to the ground. Twenty thousand miracles took place. Due to Reverend Branham's weakened condition, he found it hard to remain standing; He staggered and at last collapsed.

DURBAN NEWSROOM – NEXT DAY

Headlines read, "fanatic Evangelist promises healing."

DURBAN CAPITAL BUILDING OVERLOOKING RACETRACK

A well-dressed Sidney Smith grabbed the phone off the desk and walked over to the window and observed the huge crowd in procession. "Get me William Branham's room."

On the desk a name plate read Mayor Sidney Smith. He saw seven truckloads of wheelchairs, stretchers, cots and crutches. A long line of people was following, in song and praises.

Sidney Smith, "You got to see this. Go to your window. The fighting among the clans have stopped."

DURBAN, SOUTH AFRICA – HOSPITAL

William Branham was in bed and the Doctor spoke to Brother Bosworth and Billy Paul.

African Doctor, "He has contracted an Ameba. It will take months to recover. He will have to go to the States for specialized treatment."

LONDON – INTERNATIONAL AIRPORT – 1951

In route back to the Americas William and the other ministers were disembarking the plane at the London terminal. They were carrying their luggage, and they walked out to get a cab. A loudspeaker blared.

Terminal speaker blares out, "William Branham, please come to the main information counter. Reverend William Branham please..."

They all paused, and the Bellboy spoke up.

Bell-boy, "Would you like for me to go find out what this is all about, I know the area they speak of."

William Branham was being supported by two men. Weakly he said, "Yes, would you, please. Rich, will you go with him? We will wait here with the luggage."

Minutes later they returned with a report that a woman from Africa had flown on the previous flight. Rich said, "They have this woman…a FLORENCE NIGHTINGALE SHIRLAW, a distant relative to the famous Nurse FLORENCE NIGHTINGALE, which started the Red Cross. She is on a stretcher and is nothing but bones. She wants you to come to her. They don't give her any time to live."

Reverend Branham, "Brother Baxter, take her on to the Anglican minister's place, and after we get back from praying for the king, we'll…I want to go to Buckingham palace, meet me later. I'll be at the Piccadilly hotel."

ENGLAND – CAB
(Two days later)

An English minister was speaking to William, Gordon Lindsay and Dr. Baxter concerning the young lady, Florence Nightingale.

English Minister, "She was a nurse, just as Mrs. Florence Nightingale, and given the same name, as a namesake. There is virtually nothing left of her. They no longer can find veins to give her liquid or nutrients. Truly, the most hideous of condition."

They went into the room where the patient was at. Reverend Branham went to her and bent low to hear her speak.

Nurse interpreter, "She asks if she can take your hand? She has prayed so long, so hard. She always said that if she could ever get to where you were that she would be healed."

The hand was just a delicate rack of bones, nothing else. The whispers of the dying woman.

Nurse Interpreter, "She would like you to see her body." A sheet was all that covered her body. They lifted the sheet off. She was a living skeleton. Dr. Baxter stared as if in shock and turned his head. Skull bones were visible. She had no breast, just bare ribs protruding. The skin had joined together in the pelvic area. She was weeping. The nurse bent low to hear what she was saying.

Nurse Interpreter, "She asks, if you would pray to God so He might let her die." She said, "I can't die."

Reverend Branham asked that they bow their heads.

"'Our Father who art in heaven'...I can't ask for her death when she has been so dutiful to trust for her life. My Father, hear me, in the name of thy Son, Jesus, I pray."

A little dove flew up onto the windowsill and was cooing all along during the prayer. After the prayer, William raised his head and the dove flew away.

Prophet Branham, "Thus saith the Lord, you'll live and not die."

CHAPTER TWELVE
A HIDDEN LIFESTYLE - MYSTERY OF INIQUITY

REVEREND WILLIAM BRANHAM'S HOUSE – 1952

(Ages and dates are from wedding certificates) William Branham was out washing his car when Billy Paul (seventeen years old) walked up to him.

Billy Paul, "I'm wanting to get married Daddy, to a girl I met."

William responded dolefully, "What? Bump your head."

Billy Paul, "No, I mean it, we have decided to get married."

William, "Just bump your head. It'll bruise your head."

Billy Paul glanced over his shoulder confused while William Branham walked away.

JEFFERSONVILLE LOCAL CLUB AND BAR-NIGHT

Billy Paul Branham and some wild teenage friends came into the night club and moved to the bar to pick up a drink.

Billy Paul's friend, "The bartenders here know me. You like cards but in here is some real contenders. Let me tip you, these guys are sharks. Be wise to um."

Their drinks were served. Billy's second friend Jack, "Grab your drink. I want to show you to the back room.

Don't let him snow you over, you like cards as do they, that's it. Meet some friends."

Jack jerked his head over towards the doorway. As they entered the backroom there was a center table and five guys sitting around it with another four standing in strategic locations. A gambler called to see the other man's hand. Three kings were turned over. The cards were thrown on the table and the loser stood up.

Loser Gambler said, "That's it for me, I'm cleaned out."

The head man at the table looked up to see the newcomers.

Jake spoke up between hands, "Hey Joey, he would like to set in."

Head Man, "Hey Jake, sorry but it's only those who we..."

Another gambler spoke up, "He's all right, I know him. He's that preacher's son, Brannen or Branher… something. Right kid?"

Billy Paul was taken off guard and hesitated.

Billy Paul, "No, ugh…I'm not. I don't know who you're talking about."

Billy's second friend, "Go ahead Billy, sit in a while."

Billy Paul responded, "Maybe, after a bit, I'm getting a refill."

Billy Paul left the room.

JEFFERSONVILLE
BRANHAM'S HOUSE – LATE NIGHT

William Branham was sitting on the porch swing in thought and looking out down the road. A car drove up and stopped out front. Billy Paul stepped out of the car. Laughter was heard from the fellows inside the vehicle.

With carefully placed feet Billy Paul made his way up to the porch.

Billy Paul, "You still up…there…I see."

William Branham, "I try to always be up for those I care for. Billy, you are insistent on running through every red-light or barricade that God puts up to warn you, that the end of the road is hell and destruction."

Billy Paul replied with slurred speech, "No, I don't want to go there. Just rather go enjoy this life and the things."

"Ok, but before you go, (because with your decisions, you can't stay here where we consecrate this house to God) just stretch out your arms wide." The shadow of a cross could be seen on the wall coming from the porch light.

William Branham, "In this direction is a path to hell and the other path to heaven."

CHICAGO ILLINOIS MOTEL – DAY (1954-55)

Reverend Branham was coming out of the motel room on the balcony. He turned back with the doorknob in hand to speak to Billy Paul, still in bed. William was in a nice dress suit. "Billy, make sure you get there early enough to give out prayer cards. Mind your manners today, it could be the last."

William Branham met Donnie at the cars below the room. They drove away. Billy Paul (now 20 years old) was now standing at the railing watching them go. He was still in his pajamas. He went down the steps to a lower level. A pack of cigarettes were noticeably in his pocket. He took one out and lit it up. A car showed up and parked near Billy. Meda Branham stepped out in a sleeveless dress.

Billy Paul, "Hey Mom. What's up?"

Meda, "Let's dispense with the 'Mom' stuff, shall we?

I just saw the old man, driving away. I told you, you'd be bigger than him, better looking, too. Got another one?"

Billy reached into his pocket for the pack of cigarettes and eyes her. She took a cigarette.

Billy Paul, "Want to come up for a bit? You know it's a real shame he treats you with a hands-off relationship. You were meant to express yourself as a real woman. You're about as pretty as they come, you know that don't you?"

She tipped her head for a moment, then they moved to the stairway.

THE SCROLL APPEARS, SEAL FALLS AWAY.

CHAPTER THIRTEEN
JEFFERSONVILLE MUNICIPAL HOSPITAL

(Notes from sermon, The approach to God and Billy Paul's 1980 testimony – Flagstaff, Arizona)

~

Reverend Branham walked into the ICU which had all the usual hospital sounds and smells. He met Doctor Sam Adair in the hallway.

Doctor Adair, "He said he was out fishing and fell into the water, got Pneumonia. I gave him penicillin."

William Branham said back, "No, God showed me of him jumping out a window and floundering around. Pneumonia yes, chlamydia pneumonia. Just let it be known as pneumonia. I want to see him."

Billy Paul, who is now twenty, had a cardiogram on his arm and was in an oxygen tent. He had a small round ring on his mouth. Reverend Branham walked into the room and Billy Paul roused enough to recognize him.

Billy Paul, "Daddy pray for me. They say I'm in a bad way. Dying."

To which Reverend Branham replied, "Billy, what is this I see from the Lord, that you have been doing? First, it was smoking cigarettes, then it's drinking, and now running around with women, in fornication. Pray for yourself,

Billy. You must stop running with that kind of company. You have been privileged to stand in God's presence hundreds of times, yet you have not allowed him to even darken your doorstep."

JEFFERSONVILLE
THE BRANHAM TABERNACLE
SOME MONTH'S LATER

William Branham was at the pulpit, addressing the congregation. "I would like to draw your attention to the first verse, "Another mighty angel, (2nd Covenant, Angel) comes down out of heaven…He has his foot on both the spiritual shores and on the earthly kingdom also. He is master of both; likened to Joseph of ol', all bowed before him. I got 'thus saith the Lord,' I will have a son, and Joseph shall be his name. He'll be a prophet. There will be twins. Someday I will close the bible and hand it over to him, say, 'take it from here son.' Remember, the two will be so close as to deceive the very elected, almost. One is the spiritual king, the other by carnal nature, like Mary's Joseph."

CHAPTER FOURTEEN
THIRD MYSTERY, TRANSLATION OF THE SAINTS AND MARRIAGE

JEFFERSONVILLE
WILLIAM BRANHAM'S RESIDENCE

William stirred in the bed and woke up. Meda was still a sleep in a separate double bed, on the other side of the room. He pulled his pillow up and crosses his hands behind his head. A pillar of fire entered the room, and the Angel of God stepped from its light. Reverend Branham, "Lord, I am puzzled, what does it mean to be "Born again?"

Angel of God speaks, "The first covenant 'by the first coming of Jesus' was redemption of the Spirit only. Revelation 10's 'Rainbow Covenant' is the second, which brings about the birth of the glorified flesh body. Would you like to see beyond death, the curtain of death?"

Reverend Branham was lying there, wide eyed and apprehensive. "Yes, yes it would help me so much."

CURTAIN OF TIME TRANSLATION
HEAVEN'S DOORWAY

TRANSLATION BEGINS.

Immediately he was a young man again, a transformation had swept him into a faster dimension. No longer graying at the temples. He was ushered in by this voice that was just above him through a beautiful landscape that was at a steep angle, like a pyramid. At the capstone, William felt a rush of new blood coursing through his veins. The blood of the Serpent nature, the blood of the natural birth all removed and with it dark spirits were screaming, running out and going back to the underworld. Then he turned and took another step through the mist. Immediately, hundreds of people in the prime of their lives... thousands, came running up to him.

TRANSLATION ENDS.

JEFFERSONVILLE
THE BRANHAM TABERNACLE

The large congregation was very attentive. Reverend Branham was at the pulpit speaking, "I saw the Bride of Christ come into preview. She was beautiful, spotless, and dressed in a gown just so neatly, down to her bare feet. She was perfect. She became the Word of God, flesh became the Word. She is Him; Messiah, and Elohim the very one who met Abraham. He who was one of us sinners by natural birth, but through transformation was swept up past the curtain of time, into Theophany." Listen friends, "it'll take more than comparing bible verses or turning on a tape. It will take people with prophetic insight. It is as a several hundred piece puzzle, it is several wheels within a wheel."

"I then watched this procession. The voice said, 'the modern church will come for preview.' Their hair was all bobbed off, their hips swaying to a rock and roll beat. They were sexy, bare breasted and only a little strip of grass to cover the front. I cried out, 'oh God, if this is the best I can produce, just kill me now.' I have failed. I started to cry. Then a voice just above me said, 'Wait, The Bride will come again in a second preview, a second bunch.'"

"A second group of young women come out then as a bride, from every country in preview. Here they come all in step and marching to the tune of, 'Onward Christian Soldiers,' in perfect step."

"I was over on a vaulted place and all their eyes were turned towards me. It was a tremendous sight. The Trumpets were blowing and the blast...sounded like thunders rolling out. As they passed by, they were all in white skirts, marching in glorified bodies." Just then, "I noticed a couple of them step out of order and I shouted a biblical SHOUT, 'get back in line.'"

"I must leave you very soon for other lands...again, very soon. Keep the faith. Always be ready for the time is at hand...His coming departure."

THE SCROLL APPEARED – A SEAL SLIPS AWAY.

CHAPTER FIFTEEN
SONSHIP BY A VIRGIN BIRTH

JEFFERSONVILLE
BRANHAM TABERNACLE OFFICE

Reverend Branham was studying the Bible (Revelations 12) at his desk. The Angel of God suddenly appeared in the room.

Angel of God, "Come and see. You are the elected one, the Elected Lady to give birth of the Christ-child from fallen humanity into the heavenly." Reverend Branham startled and looked up at him. He was swept up in a whirl together with the Angel in Theophany bodies, to watch the scene below them.

VISION BEGINS.

The Angel spoke to the Prophet, "Only a true virgin can produce a Son of God, she will be clothed in purity from a transformed body, one which has been beyond the curtain of time and back."

Suddenly, a woman dressed in a white robed garment (Revelation 12) came out of the Branham Tabernacle church door. She was in full-term. She grabbed her stomach, her face in pain. She looked around her and hastened away. The Red Dragon hid in the shadows. She desperately looked around for a safe place to give birth to the Man child.

Church Mother, "I must find a place of solace, a place high enough away where those magistrates, sick with envy, won't recognize this as the second advent of Christ."

She glanced up and saw in the horizon a mountain which was partially covered in a mist. She moved forward. The Red Dragon grinned and licked his lips, for he knew she was somewhere nearby.

Red Dragon, "Let me at that young Messianic dish, and I shall be picking his flesh out of my teeth." He spoke out into the fog, knowing she could hear him. He continued, "Why do you hide from me? I only mean to enhance your life; to make you rich and to bring you security. This world's kingdoms and governments, and all their glory, are mine."

The Red Dragon discovered her where-a-bouts and placed a hand on her shoulder. She startled as he stared down at her round stomach where the little Man-child was still abiding, with hatred and disdain. The dragon's face morphed into the face of a smiling Billy Paul. He sneered, "I will give them to you if only you would join the World's religions. It is a kingdom of perpetual life." Billy Paul gave her a warm reassuring smile, then morphed back into the Red Dragon.

She was frightened and fled into the wilderness mountains. "She labored and brought forth the Son of God which could create living creatures such as brown bears, squirrels, and speaking storms and tumors out of existence, and to have the ability of knowing the secrets of the hearts of others, their past and their futures."

WILDERNESS MOUNTAIN SIDE

VISION CONTINUES.

The MAN-CHILD (who is now five years old) sat on a rock and listened to his mother. The lad was a young William Branham. She read scripture to him.

Church Mother, "Thus saith ISAIAH'S the Prophet, of the increase of his government and peace there shall be no end...he has no form, no comeliness; and when we shall see him, there will be no beauty that we shall desire him."

The man-child got up and laid down on the grass beside the Church-Mother, with a straw in his mouth.

Man-Child, "Do you think that maybe, this one with no beauty, could look like me?"

Church Mother, "Yes Son, it is you in prophecy." She dropped her head and continued to read. "And again, in LUKE it reads, 'For as the lightning shineth out of one part of the heaven's and lighteth to the other; so also shall the Son of man be in His day.' But first he must suffer many things and be rejected of this generation...Two will be in a field; one taken, and the other left. Two will be in an automobile; one taken and the other will be left to face the collision."

William Branham's person stepped behind the man-child and the child morphed into William's body.

VISION ENDS.

CHAPTER SIXTEEN
JEFFERSONVILLE - THE BRANHAM TABERNACLE

Reverend Branham was standing at the pulpit speaking to the audience, "We wanted to announce publicly today that Joseph finally made it."

The camera went out into the crowd where Meda Branham was holding a baby.

William Branham, "You sure took a long time to get here Joe, little Joseph."

Everyone laughed. "I will dismiss you now, so your dinners won't burn. Let's pray a moment. Our heavenly Father, we appreciate how you fulfill your promises and also how you hide things from the clever, the theologians and the ritualistic religious. Your promised Son, our promised son that came in secret has finally arrived to be that prophet to take my place, a man for the Son of Man. Go with us… God… and allow revelation to clarify these mysterious times. Amen."

THE 4TH SEAL (MYSTERY OF THE IMAGE TO THE BEAST) FELL AWAY.

TEXAS-OUTSIDE FRIONA
TWO LANE ROAD TRIP – LATE NIGHT

Reverend Branham was in the church office.

Angel of God, "Come and see what must shortly come to pass."

VISION BEGINS.

The Angel and Reverend Branham were in Theophany bodies watching the futuristic scene below them. William Branham (appearing older, around 56 years old) was driving a 1964 Ford station wagon on a dark night on an unlit country road. An on-coming car had its driver's light out and was driving drunk, on the wrong side of the road. William was talking to Meda Branham.

Meda, "You simply refuse to realize that we are married and you ought to fulfill your obligations to me as...at-least, as a woman."

Reverend Branham spoke back to her in calm tones, "Must you speak on this subject with her in the back seat?"

Meda turned to face the road realizing that a speeding on-coming car was in their lane.

The Angel of God spoke to Reverend Branham, "Come unto me!"

With brakes screeching, Meda threw her hands to the dash and looked over to an empty driver's seat. The two cars collide.

VISION ENDS.

JEFFERSONVILLE
THE BRANHAM TABERNACLE OFFICE

Reverend Branham and the Angel of God came back into the Tabernacle office. William's face was ashen. He was breathing hard with tears in his eyes. He looked at the Angel.

Reverend Branham, "So,? I... this wreck is... Meda is... When?

Satan suddenly entered the room and began to laugh. Satan, "Such a dilemma. Such a predicament. You ain't going to be able to go through with it, with that ridiculous notion of conquering death. To leave, to go beyond my grasp. No, no..." He left still laughing.

JEFFERSONVILLE – BRANHAM TABERNACLE NIGHT SERVICE
(Notes from 1961 "Question and Answers")

William was preaching at the pulpit, "Because before we had any sin; we had no death at all...and where there is sin, there is death; cause death is the result of sin. Like, say, if you were out here in the road and a car was coming down at ninety miles an hour out of control, you would get off the highway...you'd jump, slide, do anything, get out of the way of that car. Because remember, to associate with sin is death. Same as standing there and letting the car strike you. You know, if it's something wrong, that death is lurking after you. See? Then get away from it just as quick as you would get away from an automobile approaching at ninety miles an hour."

CHAPTER SEVENTEEN
ENDTIME BRIDE - VIRGIN BIRTHED CHILD EXPLAINED

SALEM, OREGON – STUDIO-2021-DAY
(Present day)

Thomas Albert was facing two gentlemen across the table. Mr. Albert turned to the camera. "We greet our audience and again introduce our Ministering guest, Doctor PEARY GREEN."

Doctor Green nodded his head with a half-smile.

Thomas, "And also our distinguished guest, Professor Jeremy."

Professor Jeremy, "An honor, as always."

Thomas Albert, "Gentlemen, two things are on our plate this morning. One being, this symbol used by the Red Dragon, referred to in the Old Testament a couple times and more specifically in Revelations twelve. The other is of the woman, or rather the Man-child it seeks out. Love to have your input."

The guest speakers all looked at each other and smiled.

Doctor Peary is first to respond, "The name given here in this text, Red Dragon, is Satan trying to get the people to accept sin into their heart and thereby polluting themselves. We know that God is holy."

There was a pause and then Professor Jeremy added, "According to William Branham, when 'woman' is mentioned in prophetic scripture as in Revelations, it is referring to the church, and in this case, church Mother. Mother, in-that, as history unfolds the former church age, it is bringing about the young believers. This dragon is, as Doctor Peary said, the devil but in that it speaks of him specifically as being red, seems to call our attention to a person used by Satan for underhanded deeds, perhaps as an informant or as a Judas."

Thomas Albert, "Are you suggesting someone in the ministry ranks and very close to God's elect? Possibly, even as a right-hand-man to the Prophet or Messiah/Christ, as when Jesus mentioned Judas as, being a friend, a buddy?"

Doctor Peary was sightly curt, "Seems that there is some far reaching surmises here. It simply is using this woman as an example of how we are all tempted. Nothing more."

The Professor turned to Thomas Albert. "To answer your question, yes, exactly so. Scripture states that in the latter days, it will be a time of delusion, such as a heavy mist. This fog is to hide the subtle fabrication surrounding God's works, as being only cheap magicians' tricks. Even William Branham's life and ministry, would have its Red Dragons, no doubt."

Thomas Albert, "And the woman, what is her death and a birth of a child?"

Professor Jeremy responded, "Being that the woman is the church and she is delivered of a man-child, brought about by steps of church maturity; The church woman is impregnated by spiritual conception by pure words of truth, and so, bringing forth a child-of-transformation, if you will. This Christ-child in the scripture here, is not speaking of the First coming, as John emphatically states while on the Isle of Patmos, after experiencing a vision of the future. This we can agree upon."

Thomas stared at the Professor as if trying to grasp it all, "Is this then, the striving of earlier church leaders and the (which struggled and had failed time and again, to produce a Promised seed of God) seed that was mentioned in Genesis three? Her seed shall bruise the Serpent's head?"

Thomas turned toward the camera, "Could this exaltation be as Joseph of old, the 'promised son'; Joseph coming from as it were, 'a new birth,' and then into power, becoming ZAPHNATH-PAANEAH the ruler over all Egypt? Let us review some further accounts and phenomena, being that it is a secret coming. Perhaps we have over-looked the obvious. I leave you to ponder, until next time, Shalom."

The camera panned out and the Gentlemen grabbed up their papers to leave the studio.

CHAPTER EIGHTEEN
BILLY PAUL'S FINAL REJECTION

VANDALIA ILLINOIS HOTEL – NIGHT

Reverend Branham was setting up in bed praying. Billy Paul was sleeping in the next bed with his uncle Donnie. The Angel of God came into the room and was spinning slowly around, casting an image of a man. The Angelic being was wearing a white floor-length garment and had dark hair to his shoulders, which then morphed into a large standing bear with a gold band of hair.

Prophet Branham, "May I wake Billy, so he will be a witness?"

Angel of God, "Yes, but he has resisted all precautions and mocked the supernatural and running every red light. He may not like what is seen."

William Branham was leaning over the bed with a pillow over Billy Paul's eyes.

"Billy wake-up! The Angel of the Lord has given permission for you to see Him. Would you like that?" Billy blinked his eyes and stared up at Reverend Branham and suddenly became more coherent, "He's over in the corner."

The pillow was removed and Billy Paul pushed up into a sitting position. He turned his eyes to see a colorful spinning light that glowed with the image of man firstly, then turned into a huge bear. Billy Paul gasped and grabbed for William Branham, burying his face in the Prophet's pajamas, "Stop it, don't let it near me. I can't. I can't."

The Angelic being quickly vanished.

Reverend Branham, spent a brief moment rebuking Billy, "You have nothing to be frightened about, you should not have grieved the presence of God, when it is He who gives life and hope for heavenly shores." Reverend Branham got on his knees. "Yes, I will pray for your destiny, for it must come full circle."

CHAPTER NINETEEN
AN ALLIANCE IS FORMED

OUTSIDE WORLD COUNSEL OF CHURCHES HEADQUARTERS

Billy Paul was walking up the steps of the World Religious Center along with Doctor Bosworth and Ern Baxter.

Ern Baxter, "Aren't you going to join us? They would like to hear your open mindedness toward the Union."

Billy responded, "No, love to, but Daddy's got me handing out prayer cards early this afternoon. He's hot about those found selling cards." Billy Paul laughed. Ern Baxter began to smile and said, "That beauty ALEXIS, will be presiding as Madam Speaker...just saying."

Billy Paul, "I could step in for a look-see. Can't hurt if only for a minute."

Billy Paul followed Ern Baxter and Doctor Bosworth through the door into the large conference room. All the main Religions of the world were assembled. At the head of the table sat a woman decked out as the goddess ESTARTE. Her gown was scant. The headdress was fish-like and covered her frizzled hair. Each person had a name plate bearing their religious institution.

Madam Speaker, "Gentlemen, I have received all the entries for the past four years and...," Madam Speaker turned her head to see the late comers, "Oh, glad you could make it on time."

"As I was saying, all entries are in progress for unity of all church groups and are making strides. I had hoped to bring this to a conclusion in 1977. Is there any here with the where-with-all, that may enlighten us on this gross delay of the Agenda 21's schedule?"

Silence.

She continued, "I give you a moment's time to repose... to inform you that I will meet with the Heads of State in the forthcoming Fall to present the promotion of the U.N., via Social Media and State mandates, also by our Religious Institutions."

Buddhist Monk stood to his feet, "Customs die hard and old customs never die. I do not concern myself with the philosophies of a new up-start, claiming supernatural powers. Should we bring ourselves to this position of ridicule, by fanciful dreamers that stand in the way of progress?"

Madam speaker turned her head, clearly not impressed, "Yes, of course."

Hebrew High-Priest stood up, "I am sure you are aware of our foremost problem, regarding these Prophets or Seers, as they are known. For, through the centuries they have been a continual hindrance to the kings and monarchs who rule to bring societal order."

Madam Speaker, "These Seers? Are they not your people? How in Heaven's name will we succeed with the Red agenda when we cannot even deal with just a single wild man?"

High Priest, "The people favor them and are mesmerized by the appearances of the miracles which they perform."

Madam Speaker, again beginning to get bored, "Since you have the floor and are obviously sure to straighten this out, enlighten us on who these Prophets be, and what miracles?"

The High Priest dropped his head a little, "Allow me to share couple stories briefly. The first one is of ELIJAH, the Tishbite. Elijah was sitting on a hill (in the year of 925 A.D.) resting as ten of King Ahab's soldiers, approached him. The Captain called out to him, 'Elijah, come down in the name of the King.' To which Elijah responded back, 'If I be a man of God, let fire come down and consume you.' Which then fiery lightning came down and consumed them all. This happened a second time and a third time. Until the third captain humbled himself and said, 'Oh man of God, which has the power of God, be merciful to me and come speak to the King.' At which Elijah did so. The second prophet is of Jonah, which controlled the mighty fish of the sea."

FLASH BACK BEGINS.

SEA OF GALILEE – MERCHANT BOAT (785 BC)

The skies blackened and storms poured down upon the sailors fighting to keep small ship afloat. The crew leader gathered the crew to discover a desperate answer.

Ship Captain, "It be the fault of the guilty, this storm is. Now be brave to appease the gods. Be overboard with you, to the man accursed."

JONAH was called topside. Each man drew straws to see who was at fault. Jonah pulled up the dreaded straw. He looked from one crew member to the next. The waves seem to grow ever fiercer.

Captain spoke, "What have you done, why curse this ship?"

Jonah responded with a fresh wave slamming against him, nearly throwing him off balance, "I am an Israelite and the Lord God's Prophet. I have chosen to take this trip in hopes of a safer journey. Now, throw me overboard, for if you do not the ship will surely be sunk and yourselves will perish with it." Jonah was thrown overboard by the crew, of the storm-tossed ship. While sinking Jonah prayed, "Alright Lord, I am your obedient servant. I will go. Take me to Nineveh, to those who worship Dagon, the fish god."

Theophany Adam looked down from Heaven (with the likeness of Reverend Branham) and in a whirl of wind, funneled down upon the sea, where a large whale like fish appeared on the waters. It then swam off into the deep to rise up to swallow Jonah. Jonah was standing and seemed to be looking out the eyes of the great fish, towards the Nineveh shores. The shores were full of natives dressed in ceremonial garb, as the feast of the Fish God Dagon, was in full swing. The huge fish nearly beached itself and opened its mouth before the astonished on-lookers. Jonah stepped out of the big fish onto the shore-side, in front of the Ninevite's priests.

FLASH BACK ENDS.

~

Catholic Bishop stood to his feet. "If you will permit me Madam, this is all very informative, but it does not account for the lull in achieving the expected goals."

Madam speaker who has had her head on her hand, perked up, "Precisely the issue. Proceed, Your Excellency."

Catholic Bishop, "I have heard of a movement which is gaining momentum during the last few years. It has captivated the peoples of the world with notions of the miraculous and supernatural healings, in Jesus's name. Everywhere, I am hearing of this Evangelist going about and spouting tales of deliverance. He is a bold rascal. He speaks out against the established order of Denominational system and five-fold Ministry, as anti-God."

Madam speaker, "Gentlemen."

An angry face of the Red Dragon was seen, then quickly morphed back into the Madam Speaker – her smile carnivorous.

"Whether it be all fanciful dribble of an egotistical bigot or the spouting tales of a dreamer, to be left alone without reprimand or punishment, is to bring its promotion. Who is this...ringleader? And don't start in with Oral Roberts or Graham. Graham has only six letters, which is the letter of man. They both are in complete compliance to the One World Order and WCOC.

Madam Speaker gave a little laugh, "Something similar to Revelations 12:3, we must destroy the Seed of the

Woman and his message to the Native Tribes and peoples."

Catholic Bishop, "He is from the U.S., by the name of William Branham."

Madam Speaker, "Awe, now we are getting somewhere. And is there anyone present who has knowledge of this William Branham?"

Pause. Billy Paul slumped down in his seat and fumbled with his tie. Doctor Bosworth looked over to Billy Paul.

Doctor Bosworth, "I do, your ladyship."

He stood, "But, if I may speak freely? Even though he is a bit forward in address, he is of no real consequence or threat. He presents himself as quite a loving person, with genuine feelings for the people. He believes himself to be a prophet of sorts and speaks for God. He is really quite harmless with very poor grammar and very little sponsorship. Financially, he is a pauper."

Madam Speaker, "Doctor Bosworth, I find your report rather contradictory. It seems you have some type of regard towards this William Branham. You state the world's demands for him, yet you say he is harmless? You should rethink your position of allegiance with the Committee. Need I say more? What the Red Dragon is calling for is a person of persuasion, a real warrior sweeping the nations with flattery and other powers to gain the people's confidence. A 'slick shark' if you will."

Doctor Bosworth nervously responded, "If I may, I recommend that one from his own family, one who has traveled, ate and slept with him, worked in the ministry with him."

Billy Paul sat up tall with a proud demeanor.

Doctor Bosworth, "As you say, to win the confidence of the masses."

WCOC HEADQUARTERS – PRIVATE OFFICE

Billy Paul, Doctor Bosworth and Doctor Peary stepped into the office.

Doctor Peary, "What the spokeswoman is requiring is for Billy Paul to share with this board the personal information of Branham that only a family member may provide."

Billy Paul nodded his head. "Such as?"

Doctor Peary, "Your help is much appreciated. What we need to know is what he does do behind the proverbial, closed doors? Does he drink or smoke, when in his closet? Does he have one or two mistresses? How does he get secret information of the peoples' lives."

CHAPTER TWENTY
THE POWER OF THE SPOKEN WORD BEGINS

BRITISH COLUMBIA – HUNTING – 1961

The scope cross hairs were just behind the beast's shoulder blade, the shot was clean, the creature with an enormous rack, went down. Bud Southwick couldn't believe his eyes when he got over to the large caribou.

William Branham proclaimed happily, "When we get there the antlers will be exactly forty-two inches. According to the vision, it will be exactly forty-two."

William and Bud are seen carrying the caribou trophy rack and cape down the mountain and must rest often under the heavy load.

Bud Southwick, "Wasn't that grizzly supposed to be somewhere on this mountain according to the vision? It better be coming along here soon, because I can look down two miles to the camp now."

William Branham turned his face towards him, "Yes, it will be there. Are you doubting the Lord's vision, Bud? He can create a bear. It will be there before we get back."

They get up from leaning on the rocks and headed downhill.

Bud, still not persuaded said, "Ok, I ain't doubting anything, but it better be mighty quick now."

They pause again and looked over the landscape. Just up hill and over about a mile they glass a large grizzly bear.

William spoke, still using his binoculars, "There he is."

William pointed out the direction. "That's him. Big fella. He will be a nine-footer."

JEFFERSONVILLE – BRANHAM TABERNACLE

Rev. Branham was speaking in the pulpit to an audience of nearly five hundred, "We had a wonderful time of fellowship and God blessed us with that great big trophy of forty-two inch horns. Brother Bud was awfully scared that the grizzly was never going to be there. I just had my small gun that I call 'Blondie,' that I carry to get him with."

FLASH BACK BEGINS.

The bear was spotted on a hill. They moved through the brush and gullys to within eight hundred yards.

Bud spoke in hushed tones, "You better shoot him from here and get him in the back. Grizzlies don't know death."

William Branham, "No, the vision was about five hundred yards, and it's to be a heart shot."

William and Bud circled around, hidden by the gulleys and brush cover. The grizzly stood up and discovered their scent. The shot was made. The bear wheels and charged downhill fast. It was almost upon them.

Bud, "You better shoot him again, Bill."

William still looking through the rifle sights said, "No, it was to be just one shot."

Bud was excited, and about to use his .54 caliber back-up rifle. "Shoot him! He's almost here."

The bear slid to a stop within a few feet of them, dead.

FLASH BACK ENDS.

Reverend Branham was yet at the pulpit, "Bud said, I didn't want him in my lap."

Everybody laughed.

"Now, I wanted to say that the Lord has shown me by vision, that I will get me another Bear, nearly twice that size. That's, 'Thus saith the Lord.' The Lord said one time, 'A wicked and an adulteress generation seeks after signs, and no sign will be given but the sign of Jonah.' For as Jonah was in the belly of the great fish, so shall the Son-of-Man be in the heart of his creation, or earth.' Excuse me. You see, a vision is not a movie that might take place in the future. This other great brown bear...I had placed my hands on his hips. It was already there. It will take place. There is no such a thing as a 'conditional Vision.' No, I will get him."

BRITISH COLUMBIA MOUNTAINS
HUNTING DAY – 1962

Notes: Brown bear vision testimony by ED BSKAL-via Internet video (2020).

The hunters were on horseback and had pack animals. They were moving along a barely visible trail through the heavy under growth and by great trees. They held up their ponies and stopped on a small rise. Tents were set up and camp was made. The following morning William Branham and Bud Southwick moved out on horseback while Billy Paul, Eddie Byskal and Bud's son Blaine, rode their horses in a different direction. William Branham stopped his horse for a minute and called out over his shoulder, "Going that way you are sure to miss something special."

Reverend Branham moved around another mountain after separating from Bud. He got off his horse and tied it to a tree. He then moved out into a clearing and raised his hands up to the heavens.

Prophet Branham prayed out loud, "Great God, I am one with you. I am your First Born, one from the dead nature of fallen man. You have always hid behind skins, even badger skins of the temple. Now let there be this created bear, he is The Corrector, created by the spoken word of God."

A huge Brown bear appeared upon the ground before him. He stepped up to it and placed his hand upon its haunches. The Bear awoke and rose up. William then began to whirl into a pillar of fire and raised up just above the bear, it whirled there a moment, it then descended into the bear.

Meanwhile, on a high-rise another mile or so away, the young riders got off their horses to stretch their legs and to glass the opposite bluff shelf. From around the mountain a brown bear came into view, of astronomical size. The young men gathered behind a clump of willows, to keep out of sight while observing such an extraordinary creature. He was massive, dark chocolate, with a wide golden blond band around his neck.

Billy Paul was the first to shack the magnetism, and whispered, "Shoot him Brother Eddie, shoot him while he is broadside."

Eddie Byskal still glassing the bear said, "Naw, naw, can't do that when Brother Branham hasn't gotten his, and him coming all this way to get that big one."

Taking his time to turn over a rock now and then, the bear moved in a position directly opposite from the trio and stopped. He stood up to his full height and began to smell the air for scent. He smelt man. He waved his head back and forth and then looked across the ravine, directly at the men.

Billy Paul, "It is too late for that, he already has missed his chance at him. I am not afraid to step up and take the reins."

Billy Paul leveled his rifle down until the cross hairs were in position. He made a quick shot. The Big bear screamed out and whirled around. The great bear went to all fours and ran non-stop, until he cleared the glacier and ran over the snowcapped ridge.

Billy Paul with rifle still in position, turned his head to Eddie, "Just keep that to yourself."

BRITISH COLUMBIA – HUNTING CAMP TENT

All the men ran into the tent because it started to rain hard. It rained for three days straight. Everything was miserably wet.

Billy Paul, "Wow, Brother Bud, you and Daddy should have seen it. What a bear. Such tremendous size, spectacular. You say that he separated from you a few days back?"

Bud Southwick, "That's it, he wanted to be alone and pray. You know how he is."

Blaine was cleaning his rifle, "I've hunted these here mountains since I was a youngster and I've never seen a boar even come close to that one. Probably every bit of twelve feet tall and maybe twenty-three hundred pounds."

Eddie Byskal, "It had this wide gold band around his neck and shoulders, something like ripe wheat. Just beautiful. Too bad he wasn't there. Just really, too bad."

Billy Paul, "Kinda worried about Daddy. He's been gone these three days, now? How he can stand the rain is beyond me."

William returned to camp wearing a poncho and stepped down off his horse. The rain was thick. He started to hum a song. He took the time to remove the saddle and walked to the picket line to tie his horse up. He is in no hurry and is wearing a little smile. "Oh, the bear will be gentle, and the wolf will be tame; and the lion will lay down with the lamb, oh ya. The beast of the field, will be led by a child; and I'll be changed, changed from the creature that I am. Oh ya."

Bud stuck his head out the tent and hollered at William Branham. "That you out there? Come on in out of that mess."

Reverend Branham, "Ya, be right in. I'm bound for that beautiful city."

He continued to hum as he approached the tent flap. William stepped in and moved to the serpentine heater. Eddie Byskal got up from his cot and patted William Branham's shoulder.

Eddie Byskal, "There ye be."

Billy Paul, "Welcome back, wondering about cha."

Bud handed William a plate of food. Bud sensed that Brother Branham was still caught in another world, "Best get something in you."

William Branham sat down.

Eddie Byskal, gloating a bit, said "I was just telling the Brother Bud here, of the huge bear we saw. If I was to guess it was near unto eleven, twelve-footer. I didn't shoot, knowing how you wanted to get that bear you prophesied about."

Billy Paul, "Ya Daddy, you'll never get that one. We watched him twenty minutes or so, through the glasses. Like you said that brute was twice as big as that 'silver tip.'"

Blaine spoke up, "Oh, you really missed this huge boar. Ya, he smelt us, turned and ran plump over the top the glacier mountain. He's gone for sure."

Billy Paul, "Missed that prophecy. But there is always a next time."

Billy Paul laughed. William Branham turned his head toward him. He huddled close to Bud around the serpentine heater and spoke to Bud. Bud got up and made his way over to the other side of the tent. "I believe Brother Branham would like to pull up camp and head back."

Eddie Byskal's face was fallen, crunched and red. He stepped over to the serpentine, "We just got here and have supplies for another week."

William remained quiet. Bud breaks the silence and says, "recon we ought to hit the sack so to get an early start, come sunup, if there'll be a sun."

Eddie returned frustrated to the other end of the tent and threw down a towel that Reverend Branham had dried off with.

The sun didn't rise, just a heavy mist to be seen come the following morning. Everyone was packing the horses with the large number of provisions. William walked into the camp and walked towards Eddie Byskal (who refused to help take down camp) sitting astride his mount, waiting for departure. Rain was dripping off his stetson. Reverend Branham walked up to Eddie and said, "Brother Eddie, I must've got out of God's will. You know, I've never seen a vision fail me, but...this is the second time. First time is while in Africa when those fellas were insistent on going to Capetown, Klerksdorp route; directly against God's will. I was however, allowed by the Angel to go because of those ministers setting that trap. Of course, that wasn't, 'Thus saith the Lord,' nor was it by vision. I'm so sorry."

Reverend Branham dropped his head a moment and looked up with a smile. "I acted like the 'Jonah' in this case..., but it's all over now, and we'll walk out of here dry."

Ed Byskal had his mouth open, and he stared after William Branham as he walked through the heavy mist towards the other horses. As the men finished packing up a soft breeze came through the camp and a small hole opened through the clouds. In just a little bit the men where stripping off their rain gear; and in another few minutes it was clear and hot.

Bud Southwick, "Weather is so peculiar, just snap, I'm ready to go to my short sleeves."

THE SCROLL OF SEALS APPEAR AND ANOTHER SEAL SLIPS AWAY.

MYSTERY OF INIQUITY
LOS ANGELES, CALIFORNIA – DOWNTOWN

(Notes from Billy Paul's testimony, 1980 Flagstaff, Arizona).

Reverend Branham and Billy Paul were walking on the sidewalk. They stopped and Reverend Branham turned to Billy Paul, "You know what a shark is, right? It's a predatory, one who is after something or someone. They will stop at nothing for selfish gain, ruthless; they devour the good."

A pause.

Reverend Branham asks, "Where are you at, Billy?"

Billy Paul shook his head slightly, "L.A."

They stop walking.

Reverend Branham, "Yes, but where are you standing?"

Billy Paul slowly looked around a bit and saw a building with a sign saying MAY MUSEUM. "Um, across the street from the May building."

Reverend Branham, "But where are you standing, Billy? Whose allegiance do you belong to? Before you are an old man there will be all kinds of Ecclesiastical sharks going in and out the windows."

They started walking again.

Billy Paul, "What windows?"

Reverend Branham, "Not what, but who. Billy, you're treading on dangerous ground. You must get away; out of the company you're in."

CHAPTER TWENTY-ONE
REVELATION - A GOD SENT UNDERSTANDING

SALEM, OREGON – STUDIO
2021 TO PRESENT DAY

Thomas Albert has turned to the scholars.

Thomas spoke, "Doctor Peary, Professor Jeremy, hope you don't mind me saying Professor... we welcome you both back to the studio for another session regarding William Branham, Fact or Fiction. The subject today is a phrase used often by William Branham, 'Thus saith the Lord.' Let's start with Professor Jeremy."

"I see that throughout biblical history the term or prefix statement, 'Thus saith the Lord,' was used for the announcing of a supernatural prophetic declaration. It is spoken in second person position, to show their submission to, and authority given."

Doctor Peary raised his hand, "Yes, may I inject this here firstly, that an assumption is already in motion; for conclusive research must be made to see if in fact, he or anyone proclaiming to be so, are found as a legitimate prophet. William Branham has come out of obscurity with these constant declarations, even to include his doctrine, so as, to shut down all opposition. For most are frightened away by his use of it. Who is to stand against, 'Thus saith,' God's words?"

Professor, "Then, we must rely strictly on the character and or results of a said prophet, as our foundation."

Doctor Peary, "Exactly, and according to those who went on the hunt, William Branham missed his brown bear which was supposed to be, 'Thus saith the Lord.' No brown bear, means, no prophet of God."

Thomas was seen rifling through a stack of papers before him. He lifted his head, "Umm, was there something to that statement Reverend Branham made to Eddie Byskal, concerning being the...the Jonah?

Professor Jeremy perked up and got excited, "You may have something there. He may have said it, not as a random comment but for hidden reasons. Jonah? 'I acted the Jonah.' Seems more than coincidence could allow. That great fish was a created fish, big enough to have a man inside and alive."

Thomas smiled and added, "I would like to hit one other subject (we have a few minutes left to us). It is concerning the time frame between William Branham's marriage to Hope Brumback and Billy Paul's birthdate. Have either one of you noticed a discrepancy regarding this?" I mean that the date of marriage and Billy's birth certificate is only six to seven months."

Professor Jeremey spoke up, "I have a couple quotes that might clarify the matter. In the sermon, Expectation of 1951, 'I was just married a little over two years, Billy's mother, she was taken home, and my baby... Billy's an orphan. His mother died when he was just about eighteen months old. And he's an orphan child.'" Here it says it again in the message Love, preached in 1956, "When I saw that young wife of twenty-two years old, been married a little over two years. Holding little old Billy on my arms..."

"I realize these have a bearing on the issue. This is not an arbitrary statement but have a real meaning."

Thomas responded, "I have learned that we must dovetail these quotes and not merely play them off. Often times it appears that the prophet hides things purposely by way of a quick parable or making out that he is being negligent or absent minded, when needed. I think it is neither, but he hid much by a smoke screen, often alluding to himself as being illiterate or that he was too dumb to be where he was supposed to be, or failed in something he was about to do." This word "Orphan" here, could be defiantly taken in a negative light of his personal character; I think not, but that Billy was born in six months, and that William Branham covered Hope's promiscuous actions, taking him as a stepson."

CHAPTER TWENTY-TWO
A TRANSFORMATION

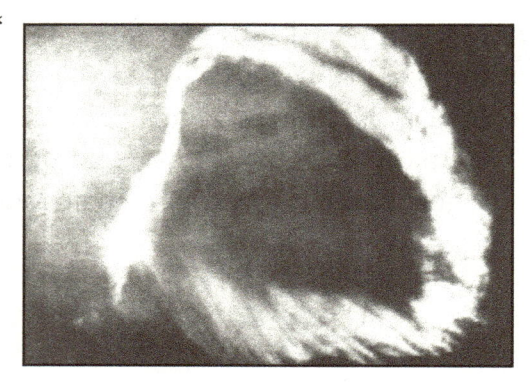

TUCSON, ARIZONA
TUCSON TABERNACLE – 1963

William Branham was at the pulpit relaying a hunting trip, "Now, remember it is hidden to the eyes of the wise but open to the humble. It is like doing a puzzle. A little here and a little there. Now listen, it will take a special class of people with prophetic insight. Not just comparing scripture to scripture, for it is by revelation that these things are given. Just wanted to bring a little report on the trip up in Sunset mountains. We were up about thirty miles northeast of Tucson and I..."

FLASHBACK BEGINS.

Reverend Branham was running the javelina down from the top of the ridge, for the brothers to kill their hogs.

Suddenly, a blast went off that shook the whole country and bounced him off his feet. It was then he looked down and noticed a goat-head burr, on my pants leg. The blast hit hard and cut the top of the ridge off, scattering pyrimidine chucks of rocks cut out of the bluff.

William Branham looked up and there was a white cloud circling above him and seven Angels came swiftly and picked him up into it. Seven powerful Angelic beings came swiftly and spun around William and his face altered to look like an Eagle and they flew up into the tornado funnel. William could be seen morphing into a buffalo calf, he then changed into a standing dark brown bear with a gold band above its shoulders. As the whirlwind slowed, the angel beings swiftly flew off and the bear turned back again into the prophet.

FLASH BACK ENDS.

~

Reverend Branham, "They said I was to go back to Jeffersonville to preach the opening of the seven mysterious Seals, mentioned in Revelations."

CHAPTER TWENTY-THREE
SUN RISES IN THE EAST, SO SHALL IT'S SETTING BE IN THE WEST

JEFFERSONVILLE – BRANHAM TABERNACLE

Reverend Branham got up from his office desk and began to recite the scripture out loud, "And immediately I was in the Spirit of..." He stepped over to a globe of the Earth and spun the globe from the left to the right, across the ocean unto the shores of the United States. "And behold, the Angel of God said, 'Come and see.'"

VISION BEGINS.

HEAVEN'S THRONE ROOM

Reverend Branham was swept from the room in a whirl.

A star appeared burning ever brightly in the distance. As William approached its glory, he discovered that the brilliance was that of a mighty throne. The throne was set in Heaven and the one which sat there upon was to look upon as Jasper and a rainbow was over his head, like that to the color of Emerald. The throne descended and sat upon seven tall peaks, with North America as its base. The face and shoulders of him who sat there morphed into four great beasts. Firstly, into a lion, then into a white buffalo calf, then into that of the giant brown bear, the last was the face of William Branham but he had wings of a great eagle.

VISION ENDS.

~

Reverend Branham blinked his eyes and continued reading Revelations chapter five: "And I saw in the hand of him who sat on this Throne, was a book written within, containing seven mysteries. And also, hidden on the backside of... backside of the book were seven additional secrets, yet to be revealed."

FLASH BACK BEGINS.

ROMAN QUARANTINE ISLAND
PATMOS – DAY 70 A.D.

JOHN, THE REVELATOR is in his seventy-eighth year and is heard weeping. He stood up and dropped the parchment onto the rock, that he was sitting at. He paced a moment then stopped short as the clouds rolled back. He looked up into the heavens and saw a mighty Angel with a flaming sword.

Mighty Angel, "Who is worthy and who is qualified to take the book and loose the seals thereof?"

John's mind spun back through history and viewed the many prophets and sages: Abraham, Hermes, Moses, Buddha, Maccabees, John the Baptist, Jesus, Muhammad, and Sitting Bull (Tetanka) and then lastly to the Prophet William Branham.

Mighty Angel, "Although the heavens rejoiced at Jesus' triumph, and throughout history many prophets have proclaimed, yet none is qualified to open the book of redemption. It yet remains closed."

John cried out in anguish and fell to the ground in brokenness. Mighty Angel reached down and touched him on the shoulder, "Weep not John, Behold, the Brown Bear, King of the Earth, which is the Enforcer, the Corrector, from the tribe of JOSEPH, He has prevailed."

John turned from the group of different sages, philosophers and prophets. He then watched as Seven mighty angels swept down from a ring of clouds to pick up Prophet William Branham into the constellation.

FLASH BACK ENDS.

~

William Branham was back in the office walking slowly with his head uplifted, "And a voice said unto me,"

VISION CONTINUES.

The Throne, being lifted from the sea, with the base of the throne which looked in the shape of the country of Israel. And out from the sea came a land in the shape and appearance of North America, which is now just below the Throne. A White Buffalo Calf walked beside his white buffalo mother which morphed into a white woman in traditional leather Native American garb. She pointed out past the shore line, out across the crystal sea of glass, to the Throne itself. The Buffalo Calf started out and it began to bleed as if it had been wounded. It crossed the sea to Him who sits on the Throne. A hand extended out the scrolls of Redemption to the wounded Calf which took the book and started his journey back to the shoreline. Halfway across, the wounds healed and the blood stopped pouring, and the Lamb morphed into the great bear with the golden band. The land of North America then swept up to the base of the Throne, covering up Israel. No longer the Buffalo Calf, and no longer the Bear, the living creature (morphed) back into William Branham.

VISION ENDS.

CHAPTER TWENTY-FOUR
THE SWORD OF THE LORD GIVEN
THE WORD MADE FLESH

TUCSON, ARIZONA – SABINO CANYON

William Branham was climbing up through the mountains and looked upwards to see a large stone that was shaped like a Eagle. He paused and then went on yet further to stand up on a knoll. He raised his hand in praise to God when a beautiful sword appeared and the handle stroke him in the palm of his hand. It was of magnificent silver and the handle and guard was made of pure gold. It was two-edged and exceedingly sharp.

An angelic voice spoke out, "This is THE KING'S sword."

William Branham was amazed, "I... I thank you so much for your gracious gift. A king's sword."

The Angel clarified, "No, it is 'THE KING of kings,' sword."

As he welded the sword around over his head with a smile. The sword glanced off his head. His hand went to his head where blood began to flow. He fell to the ground and writhed about the ground as a great serpent. The sword was shoved into the ground as William tried to hold himself steady. The shadow of it is as the appearance of the cross. A serpent winded its way from a crevasse in the rock and climbed up the blade to the pommel, there to be solidified into brass.

The Angel stepped forward and took the sword out of the ground, which then morphed back into the Prophet Branham, standing. As the Angel disappeared William Branham turned his steps back down the mountain toward the city of sin.

THE 6TH SEAL (MYSTERY OF JUDGMENT OF SINFUL EARTH) SLIPS AWAY.

CHAPTER TWENTY-FIVE
MORE THAN A CONQUEROR

JEFFERSONVILLE – BRANHAM TABERNACLE

The Angel of God beckoned William. William stepped away from his desk.

Angel of God, "As John did write in chapter ten, a totally new Covenant, must be. You are now more than a Prophet, but with a new ministry as, the Person of the Holy Ghost. You are now my chosen vessel called 'Elohim,' the third and final office of God. Go Preach 'Rejected King,' for surely the Gentiles will reject the Messiah, as the Jews had before them. The 'Pass-over' Buffalo Calf must be sacrificed in the evening time, as MOSES exemplified."

The Angel began to spin and whirl into a seven-colored light and then morphed into the face of a white buffalo calf, a brown bear, and then to that of Theophany-William Branham, swirling all around together which then became a Rainbow over the Prophet's head. The rainbow then funneled down into William Branham.

**BACK IN PEARY GREEN'S
TUCSON ARIZONA CHURCH**

Reverend Branham was speaking from the pulpit (the following night), "Several ministers confronted me the other day – I believe Billy Paul was there also with them. One Kenneth Hagan, brought some kind of prophecy against me, stating my death was imminent since my refusal to repent. They said I was anointed of God when under the discernment but false in my doctrine. Whoever heard of such nonsense. God doesn't honor false, anything. The other morning a letter came from a certain minister, Reverend Walker, which said that he had a dream that was just burning him up, he had to tell it. I told Billy Paul to let him come in for a few minutes interview the moment he arrived.

He said, "Reverend Branham, I dreamed I looked way up past the clouds and up there on a tall rock, you were sitting on a great white horse, white mane hanging down... A Native American Chief rode in a prance with his hands up. The wind was strong and the bangles on his leather shirt were flapping. He got a hold of the reins and pulled the horse's head around to stand sideways."

He then said, "When the Chief turned sideways, I saw it as you, Brother Branham. You put your hand up the third time and said, 'I'll ride this trail just once again.' Then the White horse and rider turned about and made three jumps up into the air and then vanished."

Reverend Branham continues, "Enough on that for now. I shall return soon and have God bless us again, I'm sure."

JEFFERSONVILLE
THE BRANHAM TABERNACLE – 1965

Reverend Branham is preaching to the church.

Sermon notes from "Ten Virgins and God of This Evil Age."

Reverend Branham, "Let me say, like when he is vindicating his presence among us, discerning the thoughts and turning his back. Like when he calls out and says, 'young man, you had no right to take your step brother's... that other man's wife, there in the hotel ten years ago. Why did you do that?'"

Reverend Branham turned quickly toward where Billy Paul was standing. He slowly turned back to the audience. "The Rapture will happen in a twinkle of an eye, the bride will be gone. Two will be in field, one taken and one left. Two will be in an automobile, (listen now) two in an automobile talking to somebody, wife or hubby sitting at the seat… won't answer, look over and they won't be there. One taken… one taken and the other left behind. This, remember that history repeats itself, even to include the betrayal of David's son's, kicking him off the Throne."

CHAPTER TWENTY-SIX
THE BETRAYAL AND THE LAST COMMUNION

TUCSON TABERNACLE – PEARY GREEN'S CHURCH – SEPTEMBER 12, 1965

William and Billy Paul were walking from their car towards the church office.

William Branham pleaded, "What is it, what haven't I done or offered you? This is the last time, the stepping across the line where there will be no turning back. We are partners, equal shares in all. My successes are yours. My name, my… the peoples of the world come for only the Word of God, from this ministry, a word of hope. True men, men of God stay with the vindicated Bridegroom."

Billy Paul came to an abrupt halt. William turned to him. Billy Paul was hot with anger, "And I suppose that you also fit that role? Don't think for a minute that I don't see through your subtle innuendos. I'm sick of being just Little Billy Paul. I'm not. I have an equal share with the real Jesus and have received his power and His anointing, to lead men and receive their honor. My experiences with the Association have taught me my true destiny, my Kingdom. Yes! What that council needs is a real leader, an anointed one; where that kingdom is to far succeed the one you promote. I shall no longer be equal partners. I shall crush your true identity."

William Branham turned and stepped into the church, shaking his head.

Billy Paul was approached by Peary Green and they shake hands.

Billy Paul, "His self-promotion shall come to a stop, I shall see to it. All I need is an opportunity.

(THAT NIGHT)

Reverend Branham was out in front of the pulpit administering the last Lord's supper, reading from the book of Mathew 26.

Reverend Branham, "After the same manner also..., 25th verse."

"After the same manner also, He took the cup, and when he had supped, saying, this cup is the New Testament in my blood: this do ye, as oft as you do drink it, in remembrance of me."

Peary Green stepped over and took up the tray of unleavened bread, then handed the cup to Billy Paul who gave those who received the bread a drink of the wine, until the whole church filed past. When all of the laity had received the sacrament, the tray and the cup was handed to Reverend Branham. He turned to Peary Green and Billy Paul.

FLASHBACK BEGINS.

JERUSALEM – UPPER ROOM – LAST SUPPER

Lord Jesus, "My heart is exceedingly sorrowful. One of you that I have chosen, shall betray me."

The twelve Apostles are shocked and bewildered.

Simon, called Peter responded hurtfully, "Is it I Lord?"

John, also responded, "Who Lord, who shall betray you?"

The Lord Jesus leaned over and spoke to John. "The one to whom I shall give the sop to."

FLASHBACK ENDS.

~

Reverend Branham then took the supper and offered it to the two of them. They ate and took the wine. Billy Paul looked over the rim of the cup at him.

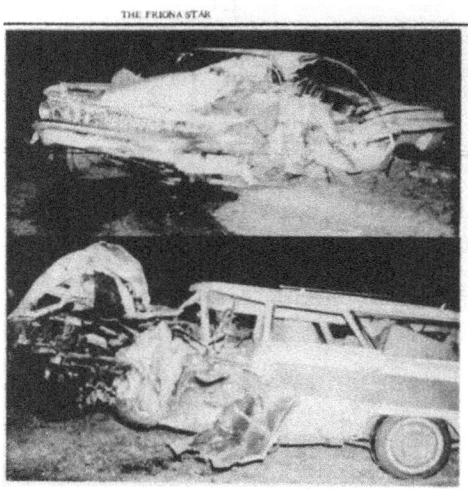

Head-On Collision Kills 1, Injures 6

Jimmie Ramos, 22, was killed Saturday night when the 1956 model car he was driving crashed almost head-on with a 1964 model station wagon carrying three Arizona residents enroute to Indiana for the Christmas holidays.

Rev. William Branham, of Tucson, Ariz., driver of the station wagon, and his wife Meda remains in intensive care at Northwest Texas Hospital on Tuesday of this week after being transferred there from Parmer County Community Hospital late Saturday.

One of Ramos' passengers, Rodolfo Melendez, also was in the intensive care unit. Other passengers in the Ramos car were Raynaldo Melendez and Daniel Cuevanegra.

A daughter, 14-year-old Marie Branham, was another passenger in the Branham automobile.

The crash happened about six miles west of Friona at Parmerton Hill, at about 8:15 p.m. Saturday. Both cars were demolished, and it took more than two hours to clear the wreckage.

Units of the Friona Volunteer Fire Department were summoned to assist in removing the wreck victims from the vehicles.

Ramos was dead on arrival at the local hospital. Funeral services were held Tuesday, under the direction of Claborn Funeral Home.

Light, Chieftains Given Plaudits

Coach Don Light and two members of his district championship football team, were honored by the Lubbock Avalanche-Journal the past week as the newspaper announced its all-regional team.

Tackle Gene Weatherly and guard Bob Sims were named by the paper in its "All-South Plains" first team offense for class AA players, while Coach Light was cited as "Coach of the Year" in the classification.

It was the second time in three years for Coach Light to be so honored by the newspaper. In 1963, when he coached the team to an 8-2 record after its 0-10 mark of the previous year, he also was named for the area's top coaching performance.

The newspaper pointed out that Friona was picked no better than fourth in its district, yet came back to take the title

HIGHWAY 60 WRECK — These two automobiles were involved in a head-on collision Saturday night six miles west of Friona. The driver of the Chevrolet, top, was killed. Three passengers in that car and three members of an Arizona family who were riding in the station wagon were critically injured.

CHAPTER TWENTY-SEVEN
HE IS CAUGHT UP TO GOD AND TO HIS THRONE
(REVELATIONS 12;5)

(Road trip back to Jeffersonville, Indiana)

OUTSIDE HOUSTON TEXAS HIGHWAY – DECEMBER 19 – NIGHT – 1965

Reverend Branham and his family were traveling to Jeffersonville. He was driving with sister Meda in the front seat and Rebecca in the back seat. Billy Paul was driving the lead car with Sharon Rose and Joseph.

William Branham was talking to Meda, "I can't, I won't be there, I want you so badly to come with me... but... I just can't make it."

Meda, "That's right, just too busy. That's just fine, the board is placing you as a renegade anyway. Billy Paul and Young Joseph, whom you said was the up-and-coming prophet, will spearhead a worldwide move. Something to bruise your very heels."

An oncoming car had the driver's side headlight out and was driving over the center line. Meda looked at the driver's seat and William Branham isn't there. He's gone. A head-on collision took place. The two cars were sent spinning out into the fields. Billy Paul stopped the second vehicle and ran over to his parent's station wagon. The front glass was busted out and the front left side was bent around. Meda was under the dash and appeared unconscious or in a coma. William Branham was nowhere to be seen. Rebecca was bruised, disoriented and sobbing. Billy Paul went in search of Reverend Branham in the brushes near the vehicle. He heard some rustling in the brush, and in the darkness a great white horse came running which slid to a halt, rearing up on its hind legs. While pawing its legs the horse turned and he recognized the rider. Billy Paul wiped his eyes and looked again. He then walked back to the scene of the accident.

Other cars stopped and people came running over to the wreckage. Billy Paul is at a roadside phone booth, and was speaking to Peary Green.

Billy Paul, "Yes, I searched the whole area. Mom is unconscious and the police are taking her to the hospital now, Rebbeca is banged up, but Daddy is...is nowhere."

Peary Green, "I'll get out there first thing in the morning and we'll go over everything; we'll search more and discuss how to share this with the public. One thing is for certain, and that is not to say that he disappeared or anything. I have a friend who is a Coroner and a Mortuary artist, that can make sure he's in the grave. Just hold steady."

Billy Paul Branham, "Yes, it's for the best, for all... best. It could be the turning point. He's gone. I'll take the ministry and go forward. He was just like the rest, a mortal doomed to die."

He hung up the phone and stepped outside the booth.
FLASH BACK BEGINS.
Billy Paul was searching around the car William Branham was just in. A rustling in the brush is heard. He

quickly went over to see a great white horse running, it slid to a halt and reared up on its hind legs, pawing the air. A bright light shined from off the horses back and he saw William Branham dressed as a Native American Chief. The Chief looked at Billy Paul and screamed out.

Great Prophet Chief, "I'll ride this trail, just once more."

The Prophet reigned the horse around and with three jumps, is up into the stars.

Billy Paul stared after the horse and rider in shock, then turned his eyes to the accident scene. The landscape of the departed horse and rider is now empty.   His face slowly turned from shock and wonder to raised eyebrows. He nodded his head and smirked. Turning he walked back to the accident site.

FLASH BACK ENDS.

CHAPTER TWENTY-EIGHT
AN UNPREJUDICE SUMMARY

SALEM, OREGON – STUDIO
2023 TO PRESENT DAY

Thomas, Jeremy and Doctor Peary are sitting in a circle on stools.

Thomas Albert faced the camera, "I studied his quotes now for years to make accurate discernment of every word, to dovetail it perfectly with his last. Finding the reason why he would make statements that at first studying seemed to contradict the one in previous chapters: the discovery is not in fault of God's Prophet but in our own discernment of when he would be speaking of the first set of seals or the second set, which is on the backside of the book, which referred to the life and actions of William Branham. An example would be of him calling the eastern peoples in the physical land of Israel, God's children, when he actually was speaking of (the person) Professor Jeremy, what is the true definition for the Word?"

Professor Jeremy, "Yes, 'Israel' was given to Jacob after victory was granted. It means, he who wrestled with God and has overcome. In the original application it did not refer to a country."

Thomas continued with new vigor and pulled his seat closer, "Which in this end-time, is one whom God vindicated as he who wrestled until he 'chose the harder way,' the precise way; that person being William Branham. That is just one shadow fulfilled. Another one is when he said that there are always twins at every revival. William Branham spoke often of receiving a son, that his name would be Joseph and that he would be a Prophet. If it is true that there are twins or two sons promised, then it is also true that at the height of William Branham's ministry, two Joseph's would be birthed: one is from a carnal act of sinful sexual relations (acting as Balaam apposing Moses) and the other is by Spoken Word creation, a promise son, 'Joseph.'

William Branham is such a person when coming back from the curtain of time/death, as a totally reborn child of God, a victor over death and hell; King of all kings, to receive the Kings sword. On this note, allow me to also inject a thought of what William Branham had said in the sermon titled Influence, where he quoted that Billy Paul was an orphan after Hope died and left him to William's care, as if he was both mother and father.

This is a very extraordinary statement, which if not true was at least, is a very distasteful comment about one's own child, which the prophet would not have appeared slanderous, without a cause. Secondly, given the fact that William had said that he 'was not disobedient to the heavenly vision' in numerous different occasions (referring to the Angel meeting him as a young child and commissioning him to never defile himself with drink, smoke or with women) makes me to have to accept the fact that he never did defile himself with women, no matter how the children got here."

Professor Jeremy, "True, it is our former affiliations and denominational understandings which blind us (denomination, is any organized people that have taken on a permissive will of God rather than the original spoken Word will of God before Eve's fall, which also includes marital relationships) to the reality of where William Branham was coming from. Did he do this purposely to blind us or was it to test us to see if we would stop believing him as God's absolute, stop believing him as the end-time full Word of God revealed in the Prophet, the WORD in flesh; the Angel of Revelation 10:1."

Thomas replied, "A long time ago searchers asked the question, 'would we see Jesus, where is he, King of the Jews?' Wise men still seek him today. Ooh, I see it." Thomas turned back to the camera, "It is as the Professor has notably stated, 'Absolutely, without doubt.'"

THE PLATOON WITH THE SEAL RIBBONS HAS ONLY ONE YET REMAINING
~
THE 7TH SEAL (MYSTERY OF THE RAPTURE OF THE ELECT) FLOATS AWAY.

Thomas rapped it up with, "The Prophet makes clear that the Sixth Seal is the great Tribulation, which he was not to be a part of, but was probably made for us, to bring correction by the last Thunders. The Seventh Seal is His return – return for those who can realize the purpose and the Person of the Second Anointed Christ. I say good night and leave you to 'read between the lines.'"

THE END

About the Author

Thomas Albert Short was raised in a home with eleven others, him being the middle child and had always sought his destiny in the love of truth and for concrete evidence for who and what was God. He would learn to seek just beyond the obvious status quo, rather than simply jumping in with the group merely because they were a group. He surrendered his heart to the Lord after a dramatic experience of listening to the Sermon entitled, "Father Abraham," preached by the notable Evangelist/Prophet William Branham with a clear declaration of, "No man can do these supernatural signs and works, no MAN!"

Thomas has spent much time overseas as an Evangelist and teacher to the Philippines peoples (1985-2005) as well as in Haiti (2015). It was during the last mission trip to the Philippines that God seemed to speak to him while in study that has changed his life completely. From then on during his personal studies and preparations for sermons, it seemed that William Branham was right there at his shoulder while reading the Messages. Thomas started to hear what appears to be the Thunders William Branham mentioned that were of the bible but with a clarity not given to the Apostles as John the Revelator was even told to seal up the seven mysteries mentioned in Revelations 10.

William Branham told us that the mysteries were to be given and understood after the Seven Seals were given out as they were in 1963. A quote: "It will take a special class of people. It will take one with prophetic insight. It will require the ability to hear from God. It will require supernatural instruction, not just a student comparing verse with verse..." He learned that it was as a large puzzle and that we must read between the lines, dovetailing all the historic verse with the up-to-date quotes.

Thomas is the father, author, contractor and Minister of the Message of William Branham for 45 years, and has a zeal for others to make the Rapture and Marriage to the Lamb a goal, for hundreds and thousands of people.